Victorian Silverplated Holloware

Tea services, caster sets, ice water pitchers, card receivers, napkin rings, knife rests, toilet sets, goblets, cups, trays and waiters, epergnes, butter dishes, pickle casters, salts, tureens, communion services

ROGERS BROTHERS MFG. CO., 1857
MERIDEN BRITANNIA CO., 1867
DERBY SILVER CO., 1883

Compiled by the Editors of The Pyne Press

AMERICAN HISTORICAL CATALOG COLLECTION

THE PYNE PRESS
Princeton

Catalog material used in assembling
Victorian Silverplated Holloware courtesy of
the Historical Library of the International
Silver Company (INSILCO), Meriden, Conn.,
E. P. Hogan, Historian

Victorian Silverplated Holloware
an historical introduction

Even before the beginning of recorded history men cherished silver as a precious metal. The archaeologist's spade has provided ample evidence that ancient civilizations used silver as a medium of exchange and to fashion jewelry and decorative objects. Silver, in fact, because of the scarcity of known deposits in the Old World, was rarer and more precious than gold. With the Spanish discoveries of the rich silver mines of the Americas in the sixteenth century, the availability of the metal increased many fold. European smiths began to fashion silver into an enormous variety of articles. Even such mundane objects as wooden trunks and saddles and bridles for horses were adorned with silver.

Yet silver remained a precious metal and its use was largely confined to the nobility and the newly rich bourgeoisie. For the well-to-do who wished to emulate the silver-laden tables of the very wealthy, pewter was the closest readily available substitute until a satisfactory silverplating method was evolved in the mid-eighteenth century. The poor made do with utensils of wood and bone.

Even in the ancient world, a rudimentary form of silverplating was known. This was "close" plating, a process in which thin flakes or slips of silver were soldered to a base metal. Closeplating was not, however, a highly satisfactory product. It wore poorly since the thin soldered coating tended to chip and peel away from the base. In 1752 an English mechanic named Thomas Boulsover accidentally discovered, while trying to repair a silver and copper knife, a far more satisfactory method of applying a silver coating to a base metal. Boulsover's process involved fusing a sheet of solid silver to a thicker sheet of copper by the application of intense heat. The bond was permanent, at least until the silver physically wore through. Once the two metals were fused, the silver and copper sandwich was rolled to the desired thickness and worked by the same methods used on solid silver.

Boulsover opened a workshop in Sheffield, England in 1743 where he made buttons, small boxes and buckles. Over the next hundred years his followers manufactured almost every article available in silver in Sheffield plate. The range of wares included tea services, inkwells, elaborate serving pieces of all kinds, candelabra and caster sets, as well as such smaller articles, as buckles, buttons and wine labels. The ware was made in such silversmithing centers as London and Birmingham as well as at Sheffield, but is usually known as Old Sheffield plate or genuine Sheffield plate to distinguish it from later electroplated wares. Although electroplated items using copper as a base were also made at Sheffield, they should not be confused with articles made by the earlier process, since the latter, because of their comparative rarity, are far more valuable. Little Sheffield plated ware found its way to the American colonies or to the young Republic, although numerous examples may now be found in the hands of museums and private collectors on this side of the Atlantic. Americans continued to utilize, as a substitute for silver, pewter or the somewhat sturdier and shinier Britannia ware.

By the 1840's the era of Sheffield plating had come to an end. In 1840 a patent for a method of depositing a coating of pure silver on base metal by electrolysis was granted to an Englishman named Elkington. In electroplating silver a tank is prepared containing a solution of potassium cyanide, a good conductor of electricity. Into this tank are lowered a positively charged bar of pure silver and negatively charged objects to be plated. When an electric current is passed through the cyanide solution, the resultant chemical reaction causes particles of pure silver to be deposited on the negatively charged articles. Meanwhile, the amount of silver in the solution is replenished from the positively charged bar of solid silver. Although the principle is simple, its practical application involved a good deal of experimentation on both sides of the Atlantic.

News of the Elkington process caught the attention of America's Yankee silversmiths. In 1847 the Hartford (Conn.) *Courant* announced:

"The Rogers Brothers Store which has been located on State Street and has been headquarters for cutlery as well as making a specialty of silverware made exclusively of dollars are now producing an entirely new and novel article in silverware. The first pieces were produced early this year. They are importing German silver spoons and forks, which by a new and unique process are coated with pure silver. This is an important discovery, as it is found that the goods so treated have all the good qualities of solid silver and are really much stronger and more practical for service. Wherever they have been shown they have been easily sold and the three Rogers Brothers are now making arrangements to properly take care of the new business. To Asa H. Rogers is really due the credit of this new process, although Simeon has also made it a careful study. We predict for this enterprising firm a large measure of success and shall await further developments."

The further developments were not long in coming. In 1859 the discovery of the Comstock Lode made a seemingly inexhaustible supply of silver available to American manufacturers. By that year there were 234 manufacturers of silver and plated ware in the United States. By 1869, following the boom years after the Civil War, the number had grown to 258. In the succeeding decades a series of financial panics, added to a trend towards consolidation in the interests of efficiency, gradually reduced the number of individual companies. The histories of the Connecticut companies that merged in 1898 to form the International Silver Company provide a capsule history of the growth and consolidation of the industry in the second half of the nineteenth century.

The 1853 plant of the Rogers Bros. Manufacturing Co. as illustrated in the 1860 catalog.

The three Rogers brothers, whose conquest of the mysteries of electroplating impressed the Hartford *Courant* in 1847, were typical of the individual entrepreneurs who established many of the silverplating companies. Trained as silversmiths, each of them had been engaged in the manufacture of silverware alone or in partnership with others. The eldest, William Rogers, had been making coin silver spoons in Hartford under his own name or in partnership with Joseph Church since 1825. Simeon had been associated with his older brother in the firm of William Rogers & Co. since 1841. Asa, trained by William, began producing coin silver spoons in partnership with John A. Cole at New Britain. Later, using the mark Asa Harris Rogers, he was an independent silversmith at Hartford. Before the announcement of the perfection of their silverplating method in 1847, both he and William were associated with the Cowles Manufacturing Company at Granby and with Rogers and Mead at Hartford. Both these companies produced small amounts of electroplated ware, but the manufacturing difficulties were great.

The success of their improved electroplating process enabled the firm to move from its original quarters on Hartford's State Street, first to the Old Jail Building and then, in 1853, reorganized as the Rogers Bros. Mfg. Co., to a four-story factory of its own. Nevertheless, this one enterprise was not enough for the restless trio. In 1855 William resigned from the Rogers Bros. Mfg. Co., leaving his brothers behind, in order to form the following year, a new partnership, Rogers, Smith & Co. Not to be outdone, Asa and Simeon organized another firm, Rogers & Bro., at Waterbury in 1858, while still maintaining their interest in Rogers Bros. Mfg. Co. In 1861 William again became president of the latter company, which was then merged with Rogers, Smith & Co. In 1862 the two firms were acquired by the Meriden Britannia Company, which acquired the services of the three brothers as well. Not bound to Meriden by an exclusive contract, the eldest brother was involved in the formation of the William Rogers Mfg. Co. of Hartford in 1865. So potent was the name Rogers in connection with silverplated ware that Meriden Britannia continued to use both the name Rogers Bros. and Rogers, Smith & Co. To this day, International Silver markets an 1847 Rogers Bros. silverplate and uses several other trademarks originated by the three Rogers brothers.

3

The Rogers brothers came to the manufacture of silverplate via one route — as a natural progression from the ancient craft of the silversmith. Meriden Britannia Co., founded in 1852, entered the field because of the opportunity to market the skills of a group of Meriden companies in fabricating the base metals peculiarly suitable to electroplating, Britannia or white metal, and German or nickel silver. These alloys had a distinct advantage over copper as a base for silverplate. Silvery in tone themselves, they showed less glaringly when the plated coating became worn.

The manufacture of Britannia ware was a natural outgrowth of the pewterer's craft, one that had been well established in Connecticut since the early eighteenth century. Pewter, far less expensive than silver, but more elegant than wood, iron or coarse pottery, was enormously popular as a material for spoons and ladles, plates and coffee and teapots. But it had some serious disadvantages. Made of an alloy containing approximately 80% tin to 20% lead, it was soft, rather dull, and wore poorly. Much of the present market value of antique American pewter is, in fact, due to its poor wearing qualities. Although great quantities of it were made, much of it was discarded when it was worn out. Still more was melted down for refashioning into new objects. Therefore comparatively little survived and genuine pieces of antique American pewter are prized and priced for their rarity.

For the nineteenth century housewife, pewter's poor wearing qualities were a positive impediment. By the second decade of the century pewter was rapidly being supplanted in popularity by the shinier and more durable Britannia ware, an alloy containing 91% tin, 7% antimony and 2% copper. In 1852 the Meriden Britannia Co. was formed to carry on consolidated marketing and distribution for a number of small local manufacturers of both Britannia and tinware. Its founders were Horace C. and Dennis C. Wilcox who had started as Yankee peddlers, and pewter-Britannia makers I. C. Lewis, James A. Frary, Lemuel J. Curtis and William W. Lyman, all of Meriden, and John Munson of Wallingford.

Although the Wilcoxes had had some experience selling the Rogers Bros. silverplated wares, no mention was made of silverplate in Meriden Britannia's first price list, issued in January, 1853. By 1855, however, the suitability of their wares as a base for plating was obvious, and Meriden's catalog for that year indicated that the items shown could also be obtained plated. By the late 1850's the company had erected several buildings for the purpose of plating and finishing silverplated ware. By the time the 1867 catalog was issued, Meriden Britannia was the largest manufacturer of silverplated ware in the United States.

Nevertheless Meriden had plenty of competition from numerous companies in its own backyard as well as in other states. In 1898 a number of these smaller companies joined with the Meriden Britannia Co. to form the International Silver Co.

Meriden Britannia Co. and many of the others were then operated as divisions of the parent company. Their individual trademarks continued in use, however, well into the 1930's. Indeed many of the trademarks are still registered and in active use. In 1968, when acquisitions in new fields and development of non-silver related products had created major changes in the nature of the company, its name was changed to Insilco Corp. International became the new company's most important subsidiary.

The names of the original group that formed the International Silver Co. in 1898 (including those that had previously been merged into Meriden Britannia or other

Pewter and account books of Ashbil Griswold, founder of the Meriden white metal industry.

Meriden Britannia Co's Works, Meriden, Conn.

As illustrated in Meriden Britannia's 1867 catalog.

participants) and the dates of their founding are:

Meriden Britannia, 1852; Rogers Bros., Hartford, 1847; Rogers, Smith & Co., Hartford, 1856; Hall Elton & Co., Wallingford, 1837; Forbes Silver Co., Meriden, 1894; Wilcox & Evertsen, New York City, 1892; Rogers & Brother, Waterbury, 1858; William Rogers Mfg. Co., Hartford, 1865; Wilcox Britannia Co., Meriden, 1865; its successor, Wilcox Silverplate Co., 1867; Parker & Casper, Meriden, 1867.

Also Middletown Plate Co., Middletown, 1869; Rogers Cutlery Co., Hartford, 1871; Manhattan Silver Plate Co., Brooklyn, 1877; Holmes & Edwards Silver Co., Bridgeport, 1882; Barbour Silver Co., Hartford, 1892; Rogers & Hamilton Co., Waterbury, 1889; Norwich Cutlery Co., Norwich, 1890; Watrous Mfg. Co., Wallingford, 1896; Maltby Stevens & Curtis, Shelton, 1879; Standard Silver Co. of Toronto Ltd., 1895; Derby Silver Co., Derby, 1873; Simpson, Hall, Miller & Co., Wallingford, 1866; Simpson Nickel Silver Co., Wallingford, 1871.

C. Rogers & Bros., of Meriden, was acquired in 1903 and in the 1920's and '30's International bought G. Webster & Son of Brooklyn, N. Y., successors to the Webster Mfg. Co., founded in 1859; La Pierre Mfg. Co., Newark, N.J., 1895; and the American Silver Co., Bristol, 1901. Many of these companies had well-established reputations and trademarks, some of which International Silver continues to use to this day.

The formation of the International Silver Co. created the largest manufacturer of silverware in the world, but it did not create a monopoly. The company now known as Oneida Ltd. of Oneida, N.Y. started making flatware in 1877 and eventually became the second biggest producer of plated wares in the United States. Another of the Connecticut firms, R. Wallace & Sons of Wallingford, remained independent and important. The Providence and Boston areas continued as major production centers for silverplated wares. The history of two of the central New England firms, Gorham of Providence, Rhode Island, and Reed & Barton of Taunton, Massachusetts, illustrates again the two major sources of silverplating artistry, the former derived from jewelry and silversmithing, the latter from the manufacture of pewter and Britannia ware.

Jabez Gorham, founder of the company that bore his name, was born in Providence in 1792. After his apprenticeship as a gold and silversmith, he engaged in the manufacture of jewelry. In 1831 he was joined in partnership by Henry L. Webster of Boston. As Gorham & Webster, the shop began producing silver spoons. In 1841 Jabez' son, John joined the firm which was reorganized as Jabez Gorham & Son. John began the arduous task of accommodating the firm to the industrial revolution. Over the next decade he converted the business from a small shop hammering out silver by hand, as had been done for generations, to a factory in which many of the processes were performed by machine. Gorham became the largest producer of solid silverware in the world. In 1863, because of the wartime shortage of silver, Gorham converted much of its manufacturing capacity to silverplate. It continues to this day as one of the great names in the production of American sterling and silverplate.

Reed & Barton's origins in the manufacture of silverplate go back to 1824. In that year Isaac Babbitt, who had established a small shop selling pewter and repairing watches, began the manufacture of Britannia ware. Among the artisans he employed were Henry Reed and Charles Barton. In 1835 the pair became the principals in the company and began marketing its products under their names. In the 1850's, as the techniques of electroplating became widely disseminated, the company began silverplating its wares. It, too, remains one of the major American producers of silverware.

Although the success of the major manufacturers of the second half of the nineteenth century was based on their ability to mass produce silver and silverplate by factory methods, a great deal of hand craftsmanship still went into the creation of each piece. The process of manufacturing silver, especially in the elaborate forms so popular in the Victorian era was (and is) a complicated one.

The first step was the designer's. A sketch was made of the article in perfect proportion. Then a wax model of the article was made by hand. If decoration was to be cast, pressed, or stamped into the article, this was carefully hand-wrought in the wax. Bronze or iron molds were then made from the wax model for casting, or steel dies were cut for pressing or stamping. Separate molds might be made for the handle, foot, spout and lid of a teapot, for example, to be joined by hand soldering after casting. Or the body of a teapot or pitcher might be formed by spinning, with cast handles and spouts applied.

A well integrated silverplate shop prepared its own alloys and rolled its own base metals. The favorite bases in the nineteenth century were German or nickel silver, and Britannia or white metal. The former, used on pieces of the highest quality, was not German or nickel or silver. Thought to have originated in China, it was most commonly alloyed of 18% nickel, 64% copper and 18% zinc.

Cast in bars, these base metals were first processed in the rolling mill, where they were reduced to relatively thin sheets. During the rolling process the metal was annealed (heated at high temperatures) several times to keep it workable and finally given a quenching bath to temper it. From these rolled sheets, holloware objects were given their first form by a process known as blanking or cutting out. Like a cookie cutter, the stamping press produced circles, ovals, squares and oblongs of the size required to make each piece. From the stamping press, the piece was removed to one of the draw presses. Here shallow pieces, like trays or cake baskets, were given final form. The blank was laid over a shaped die and held in place while a heavy metal plunger forced it into the die. A somewhat differently designed draw press gave initial form to such deeper pieces as pitchers and teapots. Often the final shaping of these pieces was produced by spinning, a cooperative process on the part of man and machine. The cylindrical tube, received from the draw press, was placed on a wooden "chuck," the pattern to which the piece was to be formed. The chuck was at the end of a lathe which could be turned rapidly by machine. While it was turning, a skilled craftsman used a "shaft," a heavy wooden and steel rod, to force the metal to flow into the desired shape. During the drawing and spinning processes, the pieces were again annealed and quenched frequently to keep the metal workable and to temper it.

After the pieces had been formed, excess metal was trimmed off and decorative borders were applied. Borders were produced by stamping, rolling or casting. Cast borders were soldered to the piece by a craftsman whose skill was so great that the metals actually fused to form one piece. Parts such as spouts, handles and finials, cast in molds from molten metal, were applied in the same manner.

Elaborate decoration was one of the characteristic features of Victorian silverplated wares. Much of this decoration was pressed or stamped into the pieces in the forming process, simulating the work done by skilled hand craftsmen. The terms used to

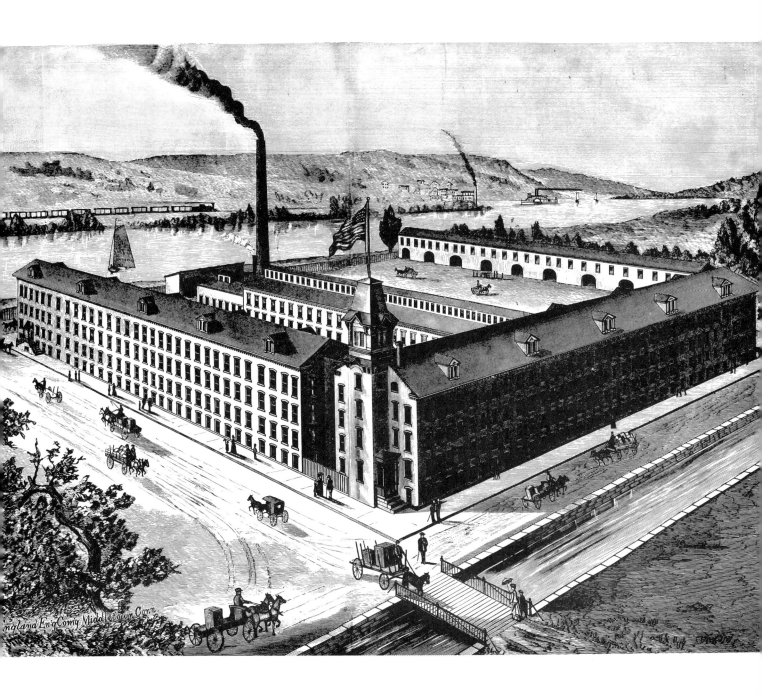

Factories of the Derby Silver Company as illustrated in the firm's 1883 catalog.

describe this decoration, even when it is done by machine, are the same as those applied to handwork. Engraving refers to the process of incising a design into metal by cutting away small bits of metal with steel tools. Chasing, which can be used to produce similar effects, creates designs by raising or indenting the metal with punches. No metal is removed. If the metal is forced out from the inside, the technique is known as raised or embossed chasing. Etching, like engraving, involves removal of metal from the area of the design. To produce etched designs, the piece is covered with an acid resistant coating. The design is then cut through this covering and the piece is dipped into acid. The metal protected by the coating is left intact while the acid eats into the exposed portions.

Two other decorative techniques were also popular for nineteenth-century plated wares. Embossing, in which the pattern is cut into the upper die of a machine-operated press, produces a raised pattern in relief. Engine-turning produces geometric designs of closely placed lines. The pattern is transferred to the piece from a stencil. An operator then cuts the lines using an engine-turning lathe.

Often several of these decorative techniques were combined in one piece of Victorian silverplate. When the last curlicue had been completed, finishing, done both by hand and machine, readied the piece for plating. Buffing and polishing were done with abrasives of varying textures, and involved metal and cloth wheels and disks. A smooth finish to the base metal, free of pits or burrs, was essential if the coating of silver was to be smooth and even. After a final scouring and chemical cleaning, pieces were put in the plating tank. Although the terms "quadruple plate" or "triple plate," used to designate a high quality product, seemed to imply multiple dippings in the tank, this was not the case. The amount of silver deposited depended on the amount of electricity passing through the cyanide solution and the amount of time the article remained in the tank.

After plating was completed, the article was once more buffed and polished. Several surfaces could be applied in the final finishing. Bright finishing, produced by hard polishing with fast moving wheels was the most common, but various forms of soft or matte finishes were also employed. Often the sharpness of incised decoration was emphasized by oxidizing. An oxide which darkens silver was applied to the entire piece. It was then buffed off the surfaces, but remained in the crevices, intensifying the play of light and shade over the piece.

Stylistically, silverplated wares followed the major decorative trends of the nineteenth century. At mid-century, when silverplating as an industry was in its infancy, the rococo revival, which had begun to dominate the design of English silverware in the 1820's, was in full swing on this side of the Atlantic. The rococo featured sweeping curves and swelling shapes. Decoration was often naturalistic, with a marked preference for the curving shapes of fruits and flowers, vines and leaves. Although some pieces continued to exhibit the classic restraint and simpler forms that had been popular in the late eighteenth and early nineteenth century, the rococo forms predominated. One exception was in communion services which, throughout the century, continued to exhibit the basic conservative lines that had been established in the Georgian period.

The exuberant forms of the rococo continued in vogue throughout the century, but they were joined, if not superseded, by other fashions. In the 1860's classic forms — Grecian vases and Pompeian urns — were once again in vogue, although usually somewhat heavier in proportion and more elaborately decorated than their early nineteenth-

Charter Oak Pattern tea service produced by Meriden Britannia as early as 1861, and which appears as an engraving on p. 52. Note the skill with which the printers reproduced the detail.

11

A representative group of figural napkin rings. *Top row*, left to right: The first three were made by the Meriden Britannia Co. in 1877, 1888 and 1878. Next by Rogers Smith & Co. in 1878. *Center:* The Kate Greenaway girl. Meriden Britannia Co. in 1886; Meriden Britannia Co., 1878; Wilcox S. P. Co. in 1884 (Dog has glass eyes). Barbour S. P. Co., 1895. *Bottom:* Wm. Rogers Mfg. Co., 1889; E. G. Webster & Bro., 1873; Derby Silver Co. about 1886; Meriden S. P. Co., 1879.

century predecessors. Newly popular were designs based on the Renaissance interpretation of the classic mode. These employed cylindrical and squared-off shapes, the latter for handles and spouts as well as bodies. Renaissance strapwork and cast medallions featuring classical or Renaissance relief groups and profile portraits became popular motifs.

There was not only a greater variety of styles available as the century progressed. There was a far greater range of objects. The discovery of ample sources of silver in the American West and the conversion of most silver manufacturing to factory methods by the 1860's had made silver and plated objects available, if not to everyone, at least to the great majority of people. At times it looked as if almost every possible article, down to the spittoon and chamberpot, was being made in silverplate.

Catalogues of the 1850's, like the Rogers Bros. one published here, were largely confined to items that had traditionally been produced in solid silver. These were almost entirely associated with the service of food. By 1867, when Meriden Britannia displayed what was up to then the most elaborate catalog of silverplated wares ever produced, the trend toward increasing variety in design and function was clear. Introduced in that year were toilet stands — silverplated platforms holding bottles for cologne and puff boxes. The specialty items so prized by Victorians were beginning to be introduced. There was a sardine box, a toothpick holder in the form of a porcupine, a fireman's trumpet, a tobacco holder, and a cigar lamp. A silverplated washbowl and pitcher set was also shown. In the 1870's and '80's these specialty items proliferated. Combs and brushes, buttonhooks, men's moustache cups, elaborate mirrors, clockcases, figurines — all were made in silverplate. The range of patterns offered in such staples as tea sets and casters was also expanded. Many of these patterns continued the rococo forms that had been popular since mid-century and the Renaissance-inspired designs that had been introduced in the 1860's. In addition, the Adamesque designs of the end of the preceding century were revived. To these were added, especially after the impression made by the Japanese exhibit at the Philadelphia Centennial Exhibition of 1876, designs with Oriental and Near Eastern motifs. Their popularity is attested by the japonaiserie detailing of many of the designs in the Derby Silver Co. 1883 catalogue.

These decades were also characterized by the transformation of Victorian naturalism into a sometimes appalling cuteness. The silverplaters of mid-century had confined themselves largely to fruit and flowers, with an occasional cow as the finial of a butter dish. In the 1880's simpering children romped on pitchers and plates or, fully modeled in the round, perched on napkin rings. Squirrels frisked on the edge of nut bowls. Toilet sets and card receivers were fashioned in the form of chariots, sometimes drawn by such creatures as turtles or goats.

The 1890's saw some new additions to the repertoire. English Georgian styles, featuring simple shapes and decoration with fluting, were revived. Cut glass with silver or silverplated mounts became very fashionable. Most significant of all was the introduction of the forms of Art Nouveau to silverware. These pieces were characterized by sinuous and undulating forms, intertwined with one another in a way suggestive of organic growth. Semi-nude female figures, peacocks and butterfly wings were favored motifs.

The manufacture of silverplate reached its zenith, at least in terms of the amount produced, in the 1920's. After that production decreased markedly during the depression of the 1930's and came to a halt during World War II. When production resumed

13

The Buffalo Hunt made by Meriden Britannia Co. for the Philadelphia Centennial in 1876.

after the war it was calculated to appeal to changing tastes. The housewife with little or no domestic help had slight interest in polishing a display of elaborately embellished silverware. The high cost of skilled labor also tended to discourage extravagant decoration. Although numerically more pieces of silverplated holloware are being produced now than ever before, the choice of items is far more limited. No longer is the dressing table adorned with puff boxes, pin trays and silverplated combs and brushes. The dining room is bare of pickle casters, nut dishes and silver-mounted epergnes.

Most housewives of the post-war era not only wished to express their own simpler tastes; they positively scorned grandmother's silverware which was relegated to the attic or junkyard. In recent years, however, there has been a revival of appreciation for the craftsmanship of the Victorian era. Although most of the silverware produced in the second half of the nineteenth century was, indeed, factory-made, it required a good deal of skill to manipulate the machines to produce the intricate shapes of the era. Furthermore, direct handwork entered into many of the processes involved in decorating and finishing. That the companies producing silver were proud of their artistry is evident in the special pieces made for fairs and exhibitions as well as in the production and make-up of their catalogs.

Collectors have, for a number of years, been interested in the glass bottles and inserts that formed a part of such items as caster sets, toilet sets, berry dishes, and bride's baskets. Although companies like Meriden bought from most of the major glass producers, no record was kept of which glass manufacturer's ware was used on any particular item. Those collectors who are primarily interested in the silverware itself find the problem of identifying objects far easier. Almost all silverplate was clearly marked, much of it with the full name of the maker. Several of the books listed at the end of the introduction reproduce makers' marks.

Plated Victorian silverware is still in plentiful supply, although such sought-after items as caster sets, ice water pitchers, and firemen's trumpets may be difficult to find. Prices are still moderate. Even though they have risen in recent years, Victorian plated wares still bring far less than equivalent pieces in Old Sheffield, just as Victorian sterling does not approach the astronomical heights commanded by early American silver. The choice of objects is wide, and a discerning eye is needed to select those that reflect the craftsmanship of the age at its best.

Suggestions for further reading

FREEMAN, LARRY. *Victorian Silver*. Watkins Glen, N. Y.: Century House, 1967.
    Many illustrations of both sterling and plate, table settings, advertisements, etc.

KOVEL, RALPH M. and TERRY H. *A Directory of American Silver, Pewter & Silver Plate*. New York: Crown, 1961.
    Good for marks.

MAY, EARL CHAPIN. *A Century of Silver*. New York: Robert M. McBride, 1947.
    The official company history of International Silver.

McCLINTON, KATHERINE MORRISON. *Collecting American 19th Century Silver*. New York: Charles Scribner's Sons, 1968.
    Covers coin and sterling only, but is a good guide to the fashions and styles of the times.

RAINWATER, DOROTHY T. *American Silver Manufacturers*. Hanover, Penn.: Everybody's Press, 1967.
    The best reference for makers' marks.

RAINWATER, DOROTHY T. and H. IVAN. *American Silverplate*. Hanover, Penn.: Everybody's Press, 1972.
    A new source due for publication in Summer, 1972.

WARDLE, PATRICIA. *Victorian Silver and Silver-Plate*. London: 1963.
    The English scene only, but useful for stylistic trends and comparisons.

WYLER, SEYMOUR B. *The Book of Sheffield Plate, Including Victorian Plate*. New York: Crown, 1949.
    More stress on Sheffield than electroplate, and, again, mostly English.

ROGERS BROTHERS MFG. CO., 1857

The Rogers Bros. Mfg. Co. had its roots in a firm founded by the oldest brother and senior partner, William. As William Rogers and Company they announced, during March 1847, their ability to supply forks, spoons, knives and ladles of silverplate on the finest quality of German silver. So potent was the Rogers name in connection with silverplate, that the firm was often referred to as Rogers Brothers even before its name was changed officially in 1853. Furthermore, numerous other firms were formed to exploit the Rogers name, some involving participation of one or more of the original Rogers brothers, others, seemingly, employing anybody named Rogers at all in order to bask in the reflected glory of the name.

As early as 1847, the brothers were producing holloware also and advertised silverplated cake baskets, casters, tea sets and other things in the Hartford *Courant* for April 3, 1847. The Hartford *Times* of January 3, 1852, described a presentation from the burnishers in the Rogers brothers' shop to Governor Thomas H. Seymour of a "large splendid coffee urn, beautifully chased and engraved with vines, grapes, etc....The urn evinces a high degree of art and skill in manufacturing and ornamentation of silverware by the Messrs. Rogers and shows that our own State and City can not be surpassed in this kind of work."

For all their art, the Rogers Bros. Mfg. Co. remained in business for only a few short years, being absorbed by Meriden Britannia in 1862. Meriden continued to use the Rogers Bros. mark, but applied it almost exclusively to flatware. In addition, Meriden pre-fixed the name Rogers Bros. with the date 1847. Holloware with the original Rogers Bros. Mfg. Co. inscribed in a circle is comparatively rare, both because of the relatively short time it was in production and because, as the 1857 catalog makes clear, the range of items and patterns offered was relatively small.

The Rogers' fondness for fine craftsmanship evidently carried over into the production of their catalogs. Their 1857 edition is one of the most beautiful of all American trade catalogs. The draughtsmanship is remarkably fine and the printing is also of excellent quality. The publication was produced by Sarony, Major & Knapp, a distinguished firm of New York lithographers, in business from 1856 to 1867. The original was printed in two colors, a buff wash over the whole plate, with the shadows and decoration in black ink. The highlights were rendered by permitting the white paper to show through the buff.

In addition to the plates reproduced here, the catalog offered flatware, an additional design each for a pitcher, ice water pitcher, wine stand, fruit stand, and meat dish; five additional caster sets and cake baskets; and three more coffee and tea services, plus two more coffee urns.

Heavy plate on best quality German Silver

Nº 5. Chased Goblet.   Nº 2. Salt Stand.   Nº 3. Chased Goblet.
                        Gilt inside

Heavy plate on best quality Albata.

Oval Napkin Ring.   Plain.   Chased.   Octagon Napkin Ring.
Engraved.   Beaded.
              Round Concave Napkin Rings.

19

Heavy plate on best quality German Silver
Stamp: Rogers Bros Mfg Co
• German Silver •

Nº 1510. Butter Cooler. Chased.

Nº 1500. Butter Cooler. Chased.

Nº 6. Childs Cup. Engraved.

Nº 7. Childs Cup. Engraved.

Best Silver Plate on fine German Silver.
(with Silver Mountings if desired)
Stamp. (in circle) Rogers Bros. Mfg Co.
* German Silver *

Goblet. chased.
Nº 7.

Tumbler.
Nº 5.

Cup. chased.
Nº 10.

Dolphin Salt.
Nº 5. (Gold lined)

Spoon Holder.
Nº 10. chased.

Water Slop Bowl.
Nº 10.

Syrup Pitcher.
Nº 10. chased.

Rogers Bros. Mfg Co.

Sarony, Major & Knapp, 449 Broadway, N.Y.

21

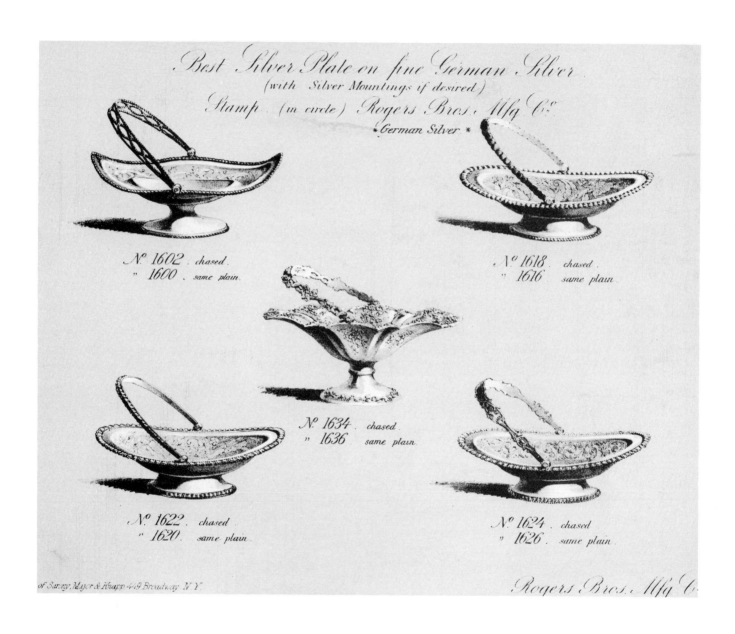

Best Silver Plate on fine German Silver.
(with Silver Mountings if desired)
Stamp (in circle) Rogers Bros. Mfg Co.
★ German Silver ★

Nº 1602. chased.
" 1600. same plain.

Nº 1618. chased.
" 1616. same plain

Nº 1634. chased.
" 1636. same plain.

Nº 1622. chased
" 1620. same plain.

Nº 1624. chased
" 1626. same plain.

of Sarony, Major & Knapp 449 Broadway N.Y.

Rogers Bros. Mfg Co

22

Best Silver Plate on fine German Silver.
(with Silver Mountings if desired)
Stamp. (in circle) Rogers Bros. Mfg. Co.
* German Silver *

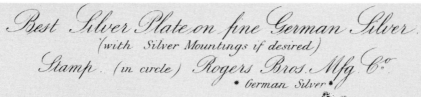

No. 1628. chased.

No. 1630. chased

No. 1633. chased.
" 1632. same plain.

No. 1640. chased.
" 1638. same plain.

Rogers Bros. Mfg. Co.

23

Best Silver Plate on fine German Silver.
(with Silver Mountings if desired)
Stamp. (in circle) Rogers Bros. Mfg Cᵒ.
∗ German Silver ∗

Nᵒ 1530. 26 inch.
Regular sizes from 8 to 30 inches.
Handles on all above 20 inch.

Rogers Bros. Mfg

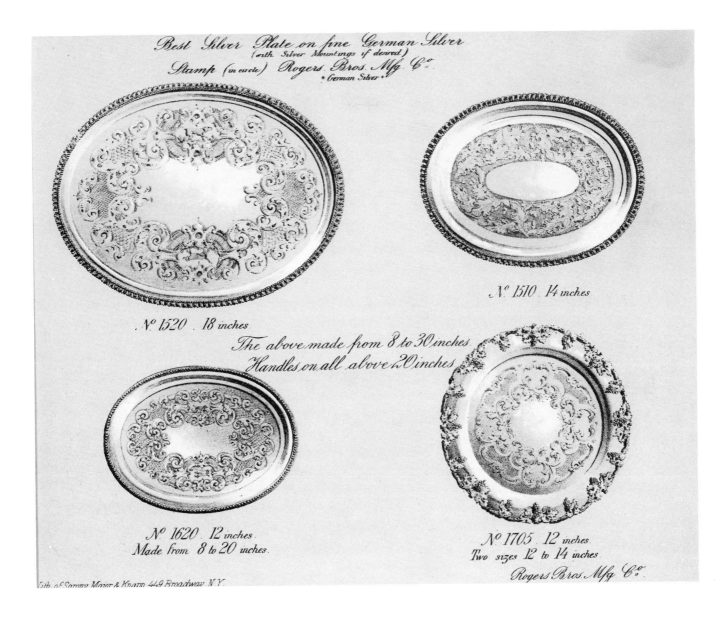

Best Silver Plate on fine German Silver
(with Silver Mountings if desired)
Stamp (in circle) Rogers. Bros. Mfg. Co.
★ German Silver ★

Nº 1520 . 18 inches

Nº 1510 . 14 inches

The above made from 8 to 30 inches
Handles on all above 20 inches

Nº 1620 . 12 inches.
Made from 8 to 20 inches.

Nº 1705 . 12 inches.
Two sizes 12 to 14 inches.

Rogers Bros Mfg Cº

Best Silver Plate on fine German Silver.
(with Silver Mountings if desired)
Stamp. (in circle) Rogers Bros. Mfg C?
* German Silver *

Vegetable Dish.
Nº 1500.
with Lock Handle.

Entre Dish
Nº 1500.
with Lock Handle.

Soup Tureen & Waiter
Nº 1500.

Rogers Bros. Mfg C?

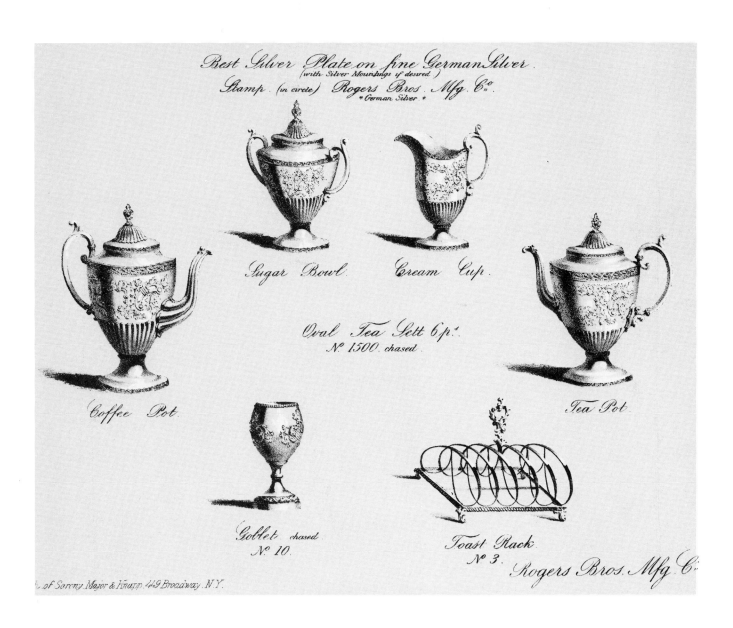

Best Silver Plate on fine German Silver.
(with Silver Mountings if desired.)
Stamp. (in circle) Rogers Bros. Mfg. Co.
* German Silver *

Sugar Bowl.

Cream Cup.

Oval Tea Sett 6 p.s.
No 1500. chased.

Coffee Pot.

Tea Pot.

Goblet chased
No 10.

Toast Rack.
No 3.
Rogers Bros. Mfg. Co

. of Sarony Major & Knapp. 449 Broadway. N.Y.

Best Silver Plate on fine German Silver.
(with Silver Mountings if desired)
Stamp. (in circle) *Rogers Bros. Mfg Cº*
∗ German Silver ∗

Entre Dish
Nº 1600.
with Lock Hande.

Vegetable Dish
Nº 1600.
with Lock Handle.

Ice Pitcher.
Nº 1400 chased

Rogers Bros. Mfg Cº

Extra Heavy Plate on White Metal.
Tea Setts.

Nº1780 *chased*

Coffee Pot
7 half pints.

Cream Cup.

Sugar Bowl.

Tea Pot
6 half pints.

Nº1790 *chased.*

Coffee Pot
7 half pints.

Cream Cup

Sugar Bowl.

Tea Pot
6 half pints.

Rogers Bros Mfg Cº

29

Nº1794 *chased.*

Coffee Urn 16 half pints.

Nº1780 *chased.*

Coffee Urn 16 half pints.

Nº1799 *chased.*

Coffee Urn 16 half pints.
Oval.

Nº1790 *chased.*

Coffee Urn 16 half pints.

Rogers Bros Mfg. Cº

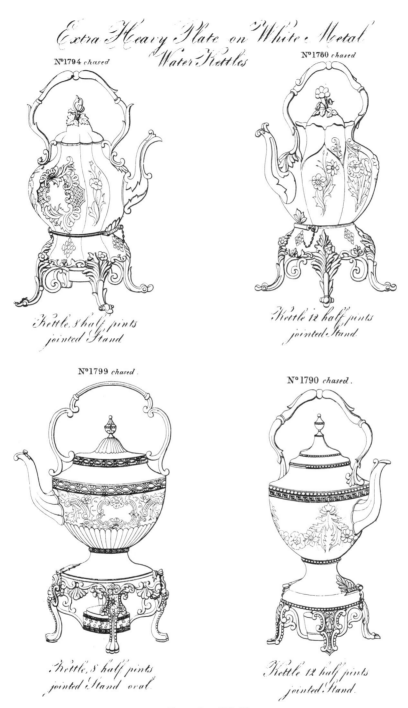

Extra Heavy Plate on White Metal
Water Kettles

Nº 1794 chased

Nº 1780 chased

Kettle 8 half pints
jointed Stand

Kettle 12 half pints
jointed Stand

Nº 1799 chased

Nº 1790 chased

Kettle 8 half pints
jointed Stand oval

Kettle 12 half pints
jointed Stand

Rogers Bros Mfg Cº

31

Extra Heavy Plate on White Metal Tea Ware.

Nº 1799 *chased*
Oval Sett.

Coffee Pot
7 half pints.

Sugar Bowl.

Cream Cup.

Nº 1799 *chased*

Tea Pot
6 half pints.

Nº 1790 *chased.*

Spoon Holder.

Nº 1787½ *chased.*
solitaire Sett. 4 ps.

Milk Pitcher.

Coffee Pot
2 half pints.

Sugar Bowl.

Cream Cup.

Tea Pot
1 half pint.

Rogers Bros Mfg Cº

32

Extra Heavy Plate on White Metal.
Pitchers

Nº 1765

Nº 1794 chased

Nº 1794 chased

Pitcher 2 quarts

Pitcher 5 half pints with cover

Pitcher 2 quarts no cover

Nº 1790 chased

Nº 1790 chased

3 quarts chased

Pitcher 2 quarts no cover

Pitcher 1 quart with cover

Double Ice Pitcher

Rogers Bros Mfg Cº

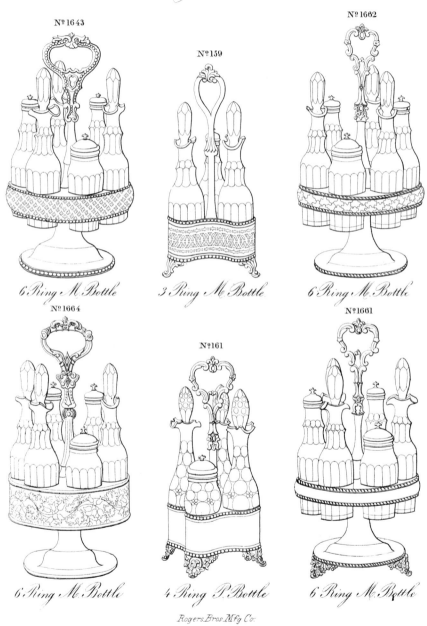

Nº 1643

Nº 159

Nº 1662

6 Ring M. Bottle

3 Ring M. Bottle

6 Ring M. Bottle

Nº 1664

Nº 161

Nº 1661

6 Ring M. Bottle

4 Ring P. Bottle

6 Ring M. Bottle

Rogers Bros. Mfg Co.

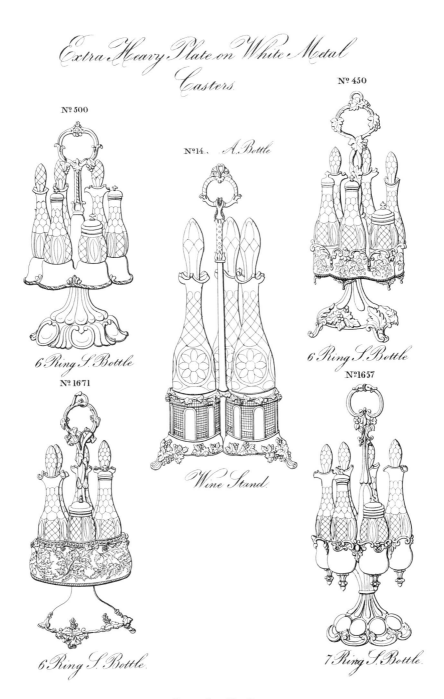

Nº 500

Nº 14.   A. Bottle

Nº 450

6 Ring S. Bottle

6 Ring S. Bottle

Nº 1671

Nº 1657

Wine Stand.

6 Ring S. Bottle.

7 Ring S. Bottle.

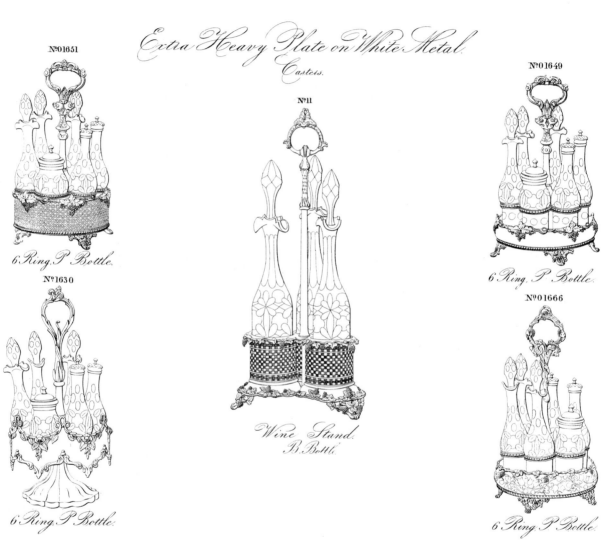

Extra Heavy Plate on White Metal.
Casters.

Nº01651

6 Ring. P. Bottle.

Nº1630

6 Ring. P. Bottle.

Nº11

Wine Stand.
B. Bottle.

Nº01649

6 Ring. P. Bottle.

Nº01666

6 Ring. P. Bottle.

Rogers Bros. Mfg. Co.

Extra Heavy Plate on White Metal

Entre Dish

with **Lamp** *etc. complete. № 1785.*

Nº 1785

Vegetable Dish

11 inch

Nº 2085

Dish Cover

16 inch.

Nº 1799

Oval Soup Tureen.

Rogers Bros. Mfg. Co.

Extra Heavy Plate on White Metal
Communion Service

Nº 2085

Nº 2070 *same with plain Mount*

Cup (large)

Plate 10 inch.

Baptismal Bowl.

Flagon 2 quarts.

Patten.

Rogers Bros. Mfg. Co

MERIDEN BRITANNIA CO., 1867

For many years each succeeding Meriden Britannia Co. catalog was hailed as the largest and most complete listing of silverplated articles issued to date. Certainly the 1867 catalog with its 138 pages crammed full of silverplated items was a phenomenon expressive of Meriden's great growth since its founding in 1852. That expansion was also expressed by the opening in 1867 of a San Francisco sales office in addition to the one in New York. Yet in 1867 Meriden was only at the beginning of its years of greatest growth. In 1878 another sales office was opened in Chicago. The company's catalog for 1886, mailed to some 30,000 customers, was over 400 pages long, and carried 2,800 woodcuts of holloware.

In effect, any Meriden catalog is a compendium of the taste of its times. The tea set shown on page 45, for example, reveals the renewed interest of the 1860's in classical forms, with its basic oval shapes, high angular handles, masks, and Roman helmet finials. The set on page 51 again features classical forms, here overlaid, however, with rococo cartouches. On the following page, the Charter Oak pattern stresses naturalistic forms, culminating in acorn finials.

Some of the variety offered was achieved by embroidering one basic form with different decorative motifs, as in the ice water pitcher No. 25 shown on pages 54 and 55 in nine different versions. Handles, bases and bottles were switched around freely to provide a variety of caster sets. Nevertheless, a truly great assortment of wares was offered, including the novelty items so popular in the Victorian era.

Approximately half the plates showing holloware in the 1867 catalog have been reproduced in the following pages. Among the novelty items offered in the catalog, but not reproduced, are an elephant paper weight, sewing bird, metal-encased tape measure, a gypsy tea kettle with tripod (presumably for elegant picnics), table mats, a collapsing cup, and two styles of cups with saucers.

Shown in small quantities were items destined to gain greater popularity later in the century such as card receivers and bouquet holders or vases. Nine styles of each were shown. Six tête-à-tête sets, small coffee or tea sets for two people, were also shown. These, too, would achieve greater popularity in succeeding decades. A modest three sets of sugars and creams was described as ware for hotels. The business of supplying hotels and institutions was to increase so rapidly that by 1888 it required a 96-page catalog to display items for their use alone.

The relative popularity of various items in the Meriden line can be judged not only by the numbers shown in the following pages, but by those that have been omitted for lack of space. These include nine pickle or preserve stands, seven wine stands, two wine waiters (sets including decanters, trays and glasses), 65 casters, six pitchers, four ice bowls, four wine coolers, 18 ice water pitchers, 16 tea sets (several of which included urns and swing kettles), three tureens, four vegetable dishes, nine trays and waiters, and three communion sets.

Also, 10 bells, five spoon holders and a spoon stand, about 10 cups, 14 goblets, three syrup jugs, 17 butter dishes, three bread baskets, four fruit stands and 31 cake baskets.

Unfortunately, sizes were indicated for only a few of the items. All prices shown are, of course, those at which the pieces were sold in 1867. It is obvious that silverplate of high quality was never really cheap, considering that an elaborate tea set could cost as much as $160.

All Communications should be addressed to West Meriden, Conn.

HEAVILY

ELECTRO PLATED

NICKEL SILVER

AND

WHITE METAL GOODS.

Sales Room, 199 *Broadway, New York.*

TO THE TRADE.

E have now been before the public since 1852, manufacturing Electro Plated Goods, which have stood the severest tests of wear, in hotels, steamers and private families, and have given universal satisfaction, supplying as it does all the advantages of silver, in durability and beauty, at one-fifth the cost.

We refer with confidence to the above facts and to the constantly increasing demand for our manufactures, and we now renew our promise to spare no expense to produce articles of such quality as will insure a continuance of the patronage we have heretofore received.

All Hollow Ware manufactured hereafter by us of Nickel Silver will be stamped and all articles plated on superior White Metal will be stamped and all such are warranted triple plate. In addition to these will be found a few Single Plate goods, to meet the wants of those who wish for a cheap article. These last will not bear our trade mark, although they are plated on pure white metal, (except the No. 305 Caster).

The goods plated on white metal, bearing our trade marks, have at least three times the quantity of silver, single plate has, and at least thirty per cent. more labor in finishing, and yet our single plate is as good as the majority of plated ware put upon the market by most others as first class goods.

We wish to call particular attention to the hardness and fineness of our white metal, which exceeds anything of the kind made in this country. The ornamental part of the work, such as engraving and chasing, we are constantly changing and improving.

To keep our customers posted in our new patterns and designs, it is our intention to issue an appendix to this price list as often as once in six months.

WEST MERIDEN, CONN., August 1, 1867.

Plated on Fine Nickel Silver.

No. 01620, with Gilt Slop and Cream.

Teas and Coffees with or without Ivory Handles.

Style.	Set of 6 pieces.	Coffee.	Tea, 6 half pints.	Tea, 5 half pints.	Sugar.	Cream.	Slop.
Engraved, with Metal Handle,	$181 00	$39 00	$35 50	$34 25	$27 00	$24 00	$21 25
Engraved, with Ivory Handle,	188 50	41 50	38 00	36 75	27 00	24 00	21 25

Without Gilt Slop and Cream, $4 00 less.

No. 01620.

Engraved, with Metal Handle,	.	.	.	$97 00
Engraved, with Ivory Handle,	.	.	.	102 00

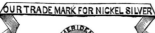

Plated on Fine Nickel Silver.

W.H. GREEN, MERIDEN, CT.

This Set is not as Represented in Cut, but has Base instead of Feet.

No. 01660, with Gilt Slop and Cream.

Style.	Set of 6 pieces.	Coffee.	Tea, 6 half pints.	Tea, 5 half pints.	Sugar.	Cream.	Slop.
Engraved,	$157 00	$33 00	$30 50	$29 50	$23 50	$21 50	$19 00

Without Gilt Slop and Cream, $4 00 less.

*Urn. No. 01660.

Each,	. . . .	$84 00

*No Cut.

Plated on Fine Nickel Silver.

No. 01630, *(Oval Shape)* **with Gilt Slop and Cream.**

Style.	Set of 6 pieces.	Coffee.	Tea, 6 half pints.	Tea, 5 half pints.	Sugar.	Cream.	Slop.
Engraved,	$160 00	$34 00	$31 00	$30 00	$24 00	$21 00	$20 00

Without Gilt Slop and Cream, $4 00 less.

No. 01630.

Engraved, each,	$75 00

Plated on Fine Nickel Silver.

No. 01560, with Gilt Slop and Cream.

Style.	Set of 6 pieces.	Coffee.	Tea, 6 half pints.	Tea, 5 half pints.	Sugar.	Cream.	Slop.
Chased,	$140 00	$29 50	$27 50	$26 50	$21 00	$18 50	$17 00
Plain,	126 50	26 50	25 00	24 00	19 00	17 00	15 00

Without Gilt Slop and Cream, $4 00 less.

No. 01560.

Chased,	.	.	.	.	.	.	$84 00
Plain,	.	.	.	.	.	.	77 00

Plated on Fine Nickel Silver.

No. 01550.

Style.	Set of 6 pieces.	Coffee.	Tea, 6 half pints.	Tea, 5 half pints.	Sugar.	Cream.	Slop.
Chased,	$160 00	$33 50	$31 00	$30 00	$24 00	$21 25	$20 25
Plain,	141 00	30 00	27 50	26 50	21 00	18 75	17 25

Without Gilt Slop and Cream, $4 00 less.

No. 01550.

Style.	16 half pints.	12 half pints.
Chased,	$79 00	$72 00
Plain,	70 00	64 00

Plated on White Metal.

No. 1950, Grecian Chased Tea Set.

Style.	Set of 6 pieces.	Coffee.	Tea, 6 half pints.	Tea, 5 half pints.	Sugar.	Cream.	Slop.
Grecian Chased,	$50 00	$12 00	$10 00	$9 25	$6 75	$6 25	$5 75
Grecian Engraved,	48 00	11 50	9 75	9 00	6 25	6 00	5 50
Damask Chased,	48 00	11 50	9 75	9 00	6 25	6 00	5 50
Engine Turned,	44 25	11 00	9 00	8 75	5 75	5 25	4 50
Plain,	38 00	9 25	8 00	7 75	5 00	4 25	3 75

With Gilt Slop and Cream, $4 00 extra.

No. 1950, Grecian Chased Urn.

Style.	16 half pints.	12 half pints.
Grecian Chased,	$31 25	$28 00
Grecian Engraved,	30 50	27 25
Damask Chased,	30 50	27 25
Engine Turned,	27 25	24 00
Plain,	24 50	21 25

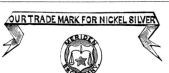

Plated on White Metal.

No. 1861, Engine Turned.

Style.	Set of 6 pieces.	Coffee.	Tea, 6 half pints.	Tea, 5 half pints.	Sugar.	Cream.	Slop.
Grecian Chased,	$50 00	$12 00	$10 00	$9 25	$6 75	$6 25	$5 75
Grecian Engraved,	48 00	11 50	9 75	9 00	6 25	6 00	5 50
Damask Chased,	48 00	11 50	9 75	9 00	6 25	6 00	5 50
Engine Turned,	44 25	11 00	9 00	8 75	5 75	5 25	4 50
Plain,	38 00	9 25	8 00	7 75	5 00	4 25	3 75

With Gilt Slop and Cream, $4 00 extra.

No. 1861, Engine.

	16 half pints.
Grecian Chased, each,	$32 00
Damask Chased, each,	30 50
Grecian Engraved, each,	30 50
Engine Turned, each,	28 00
Plain, each,	25 00

Plated on White Metal.

No. 1859, Chased and Engine.

Style.	Set of 6 pieces.	Coffee.	Tea, 6 half pints.	Tea, 5 half pints.	Sugar.	Cream.	Slop.
Grecian Chased,	$51 50	$13 00	$10 25	$9 75	$7 00	$6 00	$5 50
Damask Chased,	50 00	12 50	10 00	9 50	6 75	6 00	5 25
Wreath Chased,	50 00	12 50	10 00	9 50	6 75	6 00	5 25
Engine Turned,	44 00	11 00	8 75	8 25	6 25	5 25	4 50
Plain,	38 00	9 00	8 25	7 50	5 00	4 25	4 00

With Gilt Slop and Cream, $4 00 extra.

No. 1859, Engine.

	16 half pints.	2 half pints.
Grecian Chased,	$32 00	$29 25
Damask Chased,	30 00	27 25
Engine,	28 00	25 00
Plain,	25 00	22·25

Plated on White Metal.

No. 1941, Engine Turned.

Style.	Set of 6 pieces.	Coffee.	Tea, 6 half pints.	Tea, 5 half pints.	Sugar.	Cream.	Slop.
Grecian Chased,	$51 50	$13 00	$10 25	$9 75	$7 00	$6 00	$5 50
Grecian Engraved,	50 00	12 50	10 00	9 50	6 75	6 00	5 25
Engine Turned,	46 00	11 75	9 25	8 75	6 50	5 25	4 50
Plain,	40 00	10 25	8 00	7 50	5 50	4 75	4 00

With Gilt Slop and Cream, $4 00 extra.

No. 1941, Grecian Chased Urn.

Style.	16 half pints.	10 half pints.
Grecian Chased,	$30 75	$20 25
Grecian Engraved,	32 00	21 00
Engine Turned,	28 00	20 00
Plain,	25 00	19 00

Plated on White Metal.

No. 5100, Charter Oak Pattern.

Style.	Set of 6 pieces.	Coffee.	Tea, 6 half pints.	Tea, 5 half pints.	Sugar.	Cream.	Slop.
Chased,	$50 00	$12 50	$10 00	$9 50	$6 75	$6 00	$5 25
Plain,	36 00	9 00	7 25	6 50	5 00	4 50	3 75

With Gilt Slop and Cream, $4 00 extra.

*No. 5100, Chased Urn, 16 half pints, $30 00.

*No. 5100, Plain Urn, 16 half pints, $24 00.

No. 1808, Fluted.

Style.	Set of 6 pieces.	Coffee.	Tea, 6 half pints.	Tea, 5 half pints.	Sugar.	Cream.	Slop.
Fluted,	$48 00	$11 50	$10 00	$9 50	$7 00	$5 25	$4 75

With Gilt Slop and Cream, $4 00 extra.

* No Cuts.

Plated on White Metal.

No. 1790, Plain.

Style.	Set of 6 pieces.	Coffee.	Tea, 6 half pints.	Tea, 5 half pints.	Sugar.	Cream.	Slop.
Grape Chased,	$50 00	$12 50	$10 00	$9 50	$6 50	$6 00	$5 50
Engine,	42 00	10 75	8 50	8 00	5 00	5 00	4 50
Plain,	37 00	9 50	7 50	7 00	4 75	4 25	4 00

With Gilt Slop and Cream, $4 00 extra.

No. 1790 Plain.		**No. 1790, Plain Swing Kettle.**	**No. 1860, Plain Hotel.**

	16 half pints.	12 half pints.		12 half pints.		12 quarts.
Chased,	$31 50	$28 00.	Chased,	$30 75.	Plain,	$50 00.
Engine,	27 75	24 50.	Engine,	28 00.		8 quarts.
Plain,	24 00	22 00.	Plain,	24 00.	Plain,	$40 00.

DOUBLE WALL PATENT VALVE

ICE PITCHERS,

PLATED ON

WHITE METAL.

No. 25, X Medallion.

Each, $17 00.

No. 25, XX (D) Medallion.

Each, $18 00.

No. 25, Grecian.

Each, $16 00.

No. 25, XX (G) Medallion.

Each, $18 00.

No. 25, XX Grecian.

Each, $18 00.

No. 25, XX Flowered.

Each, $18 00

Plated on White Metal.

No. 25, X Straight Line Engine.
Each, $17 00.

No. 25, X Grecian Engine.
Each, $16 00.

No. 25, X Block Engine.
Each, $17 00.

No. 23, Straight Line Engine.
Each, $15 25.

No 37, X Chased.
Chased or Medallion, each, $18 00.
X Chased or Medallion, each,   19 00.
XX Chased or Medallion, each, 20 00.

**No. 24, Straight Line Engine,
Octagon Shape.**
Each, $18 00.

No. 10, Plain. Each, $13 50.
Straight Line Engine, each,   15 00.

No. 13, Grecian Chased.
Each, $16 00.

No. 13, XX Engine.
Each, $17 00.

All Goods bearing our Trade Marks
are Triple Plate.

Plated on White Metal.

No. 3, XX, Paneled Chased.
Each, $17 00.

No. 3, Scenery Chased, (B).
Each, $18 00.

No. 3, Wreath Chased.
Each, $16 00.

No. 3, N, Grape Chased.
Each, $14 25.

No. 3, Plain.
Each, $13 00.

No. 3, N, Plain.
Each, $13 00.

No. 2, Wreath Chased.
Each, $14 25.

No. 2 Engine.
Each, $12 75.

No. 2, Plain.
Each, $11 25.

56

THE FOLLOWING

ICE PITCHERS ARE SINGLE PLATE,

And do not bear our Trade Mark.

No. 29, Engine Medallion.
Each, $13 00.

No. 28 Engine Medallion.
Each, $12 75.

No. 28, Medallion Engraved.
Each, $12 75.

No. 33, N, Engine.

No. 33, N, Engine, each,	$10 00.
No. 33, N, Plain, each,	9 00.
*No. 33, Engine, each,	10 00.
No. 33, Plain, each,	9 00.

* No. 33 is same as No. 33 N, except not fluted.

LYMAN'S
PATENT
Double Valve.

Placed in the throat of the Nozzle to our
Ice Pitchers.

Patented June 8th, 1858.

No. 43, Engine.

†No. 43 N, Engine, each,	$9 00.
No. 43 N, Plain, each,	8 25.
No. 43, Engine, each,	9 00.
No. 43, Plain, each,	8 25.

†No. 43 N is like No. 43, except fluted.

ICE PITCHER WAITERS

PLATED ON

WHITE METAL.

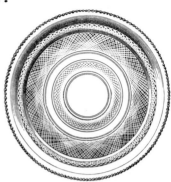

No. 23, Engine.

Each, $5 25.

No. 6, Engine Round Waiter.

Engine,	10 inch, each,	$5 25.
Engine,	12 inch, each,	5 75.
Engine,	14 inch, each,	6 75.
Grecian or Medallion,	10 inch, each,	6 00.
Grecian or Medallion,	12 inch, each,	6 50.
Grecian or Medallion,	14 inch, each,	7 50.

No. 5 Round Waiter same as No. 6, only fluted border, price same as No. 6.

No. 10, Engine.

Each, $5 25.

Double Wall Ice Urns

Plated on White Metal.

No. 33, Engine.

Single Plate.

Each, $3 50.

No. 1860.

1 Gallon, Engine, each,	$26 00.
1 Gallon, Plain, each,	23 00.
2 Gallons, Engine or Chased, each,	50 00.
2 Gallons, Plain, each,	45 00.

No. 1808.

Each, $30 00.

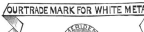

Plated on White Metal.

No. 4100, Chased.

10 half pints.

No. 3100, Chased.

10 half pints.

No. 3100, Chased.

8 half pints.

Chased,	10 half pints,	each,	$11 25.
Chased,	8 half pints,	each,	10 00.
Chased,	6 half pints,	each,	8 75.
Chased,	3 half pints,	each,	6 00.

No. 4200 Engine Turned.

8 half pints.

No. 3200, Engine Turned.

10 half pints.

No. 3200, Engine Turned.

6 half pints.

Engine,	10 half pints, each,	$12 75.		Engine,	10 half pints,	each,	$12 75.
Engine,	8 half pints, each,	11 25.		Engine,	8 half pints,	each,	11 25.
Engine,	6 half pints, each,	10 50.		Engine,	6 half pints,	each,	10 50.
Engine,	3 half pints, each,	6 00.		Engine,	3 half pints,	each,	6 00.
Plain,	10 half pints, each,	10 50.		Plain,	10 half pints,	each,	10 50.
Plain,	8 half pints, each,	9 25.		Plain,	8 half pints,	each,	9 50.
Plain,	6 half pints, each,	8 00.		Plain,	6 half pints,	each,	8 00.
Plain,	3 half pints, each,	5 00.		Plain,	3 half pints,	each,	5 00.

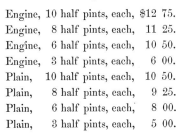

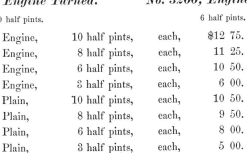

C A S T E R S

PLATED ON
N I C K E L   S I L V E R.

No. 0722, (Oval Shape).
6 Bottles. Each, $38 00.

No. 04188.
6 No. 200 Bottles. Each, $26 50.

No. 04117.
6 No. 300 Bottles. Each, $22 50.

No. 04194.
With 6 No. 300 or 200 Bottles.
Each, $27 25.

No. 01986.
6 No. 400 Bottles. Each, $22 00.
With No. 300 or 200 Bottles. Each, $18 50.

*No. 01985.
5 No. 400 Bottles. Each, $19 50.
With No. 300 or 200 Bottles. Each, $16 25.

*No. 01984.
4 No. 400 Bottles. Each, $17 00.
With No. 300 or 200 Bottles. Each, $14 50.

* Very nearly the same in appearance as No. 01986.

No. 0704.
With No. 300 Bottles.
Each, $20 75.

All Goods bearing our Trade Marks
are Triple Plate.

Plated on Nickel Silver.

No. 0715.
6 No. 500 Bottles. Each, $36 75.
With No. 300 Bottles. Each, $33 50.

No. 0719.
6 No. 700 Bottles. Each, $36 00.
With No. 300 Bottles. Each, $32 75.

No. 0720.
6 No. 800 Bottles. Each, $44 50.

No. 0708.
6 No. 300 Bottles. Each, $32 00.
With No. 400 Bottles. Each, $35 25.

No. 0709.
6 No. 400 Bottles. Each, $36 00.
With No. 300 or 200 Bottles. Each, $32 75.

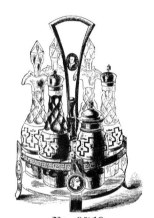

No. 0710.
6 No. 500 Bottles. Each, $36 75.
With No. 300 Bottles. Each, $33 50.

No. 0705.
6 No. 300 Bottles. Each, $30 00.

No. 04118.
No. 200 Bottles. Each, $28 00.

No. 04119.
6 No. 300 Bottles. Each, $28 00.

Plated on Nickel Silver.

No. 01976.
6 No. 100 Bottles. Each, $26 00.
Handle of this Caster made of White Metal.

No. 01975.
7 No. 100 Bottles. Each, $30 00.
This Caster has White Metal feet.

No. 01970.
6 No. 100 Bottles. Each, $22 00.
This Caster has White Metal feet.

No. 04168.
6 No. 70½ Bottles. Each, $22 75.
With No. 54 Bottles. Each, $24 00.
With No. 300 Bottles. Each, 25 25.

No. 04116.
6 No. 300 Bottles. Each, $26 25.
6 No. 54 Bottles. Each, 25 00.
6 No. 70½ Bottles. Each, 23 75.

No. 0300.
6 No. 300 Bottles. Each, $22 00.
With No. 54 Bottles. Each, $20 75.
With No. 70½ Bottles. Each, 19 50.

No. 04199.
With 6 No. 300 Bottles. Each, $28 00.

No. 04110.
4 No. 1970 Bottles. Each, $16 00.
No. 04199½ same as No. 04199, except Grecian border instead of Beaded. Each, $28 00.

No. 04184.
6 Best Bottles. Each, $24 00.

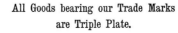

Plated on Nickel Silver.

No. 04190.
6 No. 72 Bottles.   Each, $25 50.
With No. 54 Bottles.   Each, $26 75.
With No. 300 Bottles.   Each, 28 00.

No. 04180.
6 No. 74 Bottles.   Each, $21 50.
With No. 300 Bottles.   Each, $24 00.

No. 04172.
With 6 No. 200 Bottles.   Each, $24 00.
With No. 54 Bottles.   Each, $22 75.
With No. 74 Bottles.   Each, 21 50.

No. 04196.
6 No. 300 Bottles.   Each, $27 25.
With No. 54 Bottles.   Each, $26 00.
With No. 74 Bottles.   Each, 24 75.

No. 04120.
With 6 No. 300 Bottles.   Each, $24 00.
With No. 54 Bottles.   Each, $22 75.
With No. 74 Bottles.   Each, 21 50.

No. 04162.
6 No. 200 Bottles.   Each, $22 50.
With No. 54 Bottles.   Each, 21 25.
With No. 74 Bottles.   Each, 20 00.

No. 04177.
With 6 No. 300 Bottles.   Each, $24 00.

No. 04184.
4 Best Bottles.   Each, $20 00.

No. 04160.
2 Jugs.   Each, $23 25.
3 Jugs.   Each, 27 25.

BREAKFAST CASTERS

PLATED ON

NICKEL SILVER.

No. 0721.
4 Bottles, with 2 Gilt Salts.   Each, $20 50.

No. 01982.
4 Best Bottles.   Each, $12 25.

No. 01982.
3 Best Bottles.   Each, $10 00.

No. 01979.
3 Wreath Bottles.   Each, $10 50.

No. 04144.
4 Bottles, with 4 Gilt Egg Cups.
Each, $22 00.

No. 01981.
3 No. 81 Bottles.   Each, $5 50.

No. 01981.
4 No. 81 Bottles.   Each, $7 25.

No. 01970.
4 Best Bottles.   Each, $13 25.
This Caster has White Metal feet.

No. 01980.
3 Best Bottles.   Each, $11 00.
This Caster has White Metal feet.

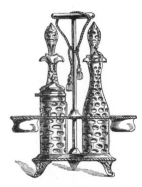

No. 04104.
4 Bottles and 2 Gilt Salts.
With No. 300 Bottles.   Each, $18 75.

BREAKFAST CASTERS

PLATED ON

WHITE METAL.

PATENTED.
No. 169.
4 Wreath Bottles, with 2 Salts and Spoons.
Each, $9 25.

PATENTED.
No. 166.
4 Wreath Bottles.
Each, $7 00.

PATENTED.
No. 166.
3 Wreath Bottles.
Each, $6 00.

PATENTED.
No. 168.
3 Wreath Bottles, with Salt.
Each, $7 25.

No. 1964.
4 Bottles, Ruby and Blue Salts,
Gilt Albata Spoons.   Each, $8 50.

No. 1965.
4 Ground Bottles.
Each, $7 00.
3 Bottles.   Each, $6 00.

No. 1965 1-2.
3 Bottles and Salt.
Each, $7 00.
With 2 Bottles.   Each, $6 00.

No. 1966.
3 Bottles, Ruby or Blue Salt, Gilt Spoon.
Each, $7 25.

No. 130.
3 Flowered Bottles.
Each, $6 50.

No. 172.
2 Bottles, Salts and Spoons.
Each, $6 00.

THE FOLLOWING

BREAKFAST CASTERS

ARE SINGLE PLATE, AND DO NOT BEAR OUR TRADE MARK.

No. 1968.
4 Ground or Wreath Bottles, Salts and Spoons.
Each, $6 00.

No. 1968.
4 No. 43 Bottles.
Each, $5 75.

* No. 1967.
Each, $6 00.

No. 165.
4 No. 43 Bottles.
Each, $4 00.

No. 165.
3 Wreath or Ground Bottles.
Each, $4 25.
With 4 Wreath or Ground Bottles.   Each, $4 50.

No. 165 1-2.
3 Ground or Wreath Bottles, with Salt.
Each, $4 50.

No. 165.
3 No. 43 Bottles.
Each, $3 50.

No. 1960.
4 No. 1 Bottles.   Each, $6 50.

No. 1960.
3 No. 2 Bottles.   Each, $5 25.

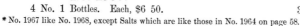

* No. 1967 like No. 1968, except Salts which are like those in No. 1964 on page 58.

Plated on White Metal.

No. 2034.

6 No. 3½ Bottles.   Each, $7 75.

With No. 74 Bottles.   Each, $8 50.

No. 2028.

6 No. 2½ Bottles.   Each, $7 50.

With No. 70½ Bottles.   Each, $8 25.

No. 520.

6 No. 1 Bottles.   Each, $7 50.

With 5 No. 1 Bottles.   Each, $6 75.

No. 1659.

6 No. 53 Bottles.   Each, $18 00.

No. 1657.

7 No. 53 Bottles.   Each, $19 00.

No. 125.

With 6 No. 54 Bottles.   Each, $17 25.

Plated on White Metal.

No. 3, Engine.

7 Bottles.   Each, $22 75.

Bottom to No. 3.

Can be used as Fruit Stand.

Top to No. 3.

Can be used as Basket Caster.

No. 1700.

6 No. 2½ Bottles.   Each, $10 50.

No. 1860, Chased or Engine.

6 No. 100 Bottles.   Each, $40 00.

Top to No. 1860.

Bottom to No. 1860.

Used as an Egg Stand.

No. 578.

6 No. 2½ Bottles.   Each, $11 00.

Plated on White Metal.

No. 11.

6 No. 6 Bottles.   Each, $15 00.

No. 33.

6 No. 75 Bottles.   Each, $12 00.

No. 44.

6 No. 70 Bottles.   Each, $12 00.

No. 2500.

6 No. 59 Bottles.   Each, $16 50.

Revolves inside the Band.

No. 2520.

6 No. 59 Bottles.   Each, $16 00.

Band revolves.

No. 2530.

6 No. 2½ Bottles.   Each, $13 00.

Plated on White Metal.

No. 2580.

6 No. 53 or 54 Bottles.   Each, $15 00.

No. 133.

6 No. 70½ Bottles.   Each, $13 00.

No. 134.

6 No. 300 Bottles.   Each, $16 50.

With 6 No. 54 Bottles.   Each, $15 25.

With 6 No. 70½ Bottles.   Each $14 00.

No. 133, Grecian Chased or Medallion.

With No. 300 Bottles.   Each, $16 50.

With No. 54 Bottles.   Each, 15 25.

With No. 70½ Bottles.   Each, 14 00.

No. 2590.

6 No. 34 or 54 Bottles.   Each, $15 00.

No. 2400.

6 No. 55 Bottles.   Each, $12 50.

With 6 No. 70½ Bottles.   Each, $11 25.

No. 2200.

6 No. 53 or 54 Bottles.   Each, $14 00.

Plated on White Metal.

No. 576.

6 No. 3 Bottles.   Each, $8 25.
With 5 No. 3 Bottles.   Each, $7 50.

No. 579.

6 No. 2½ Bottles.   Each, $9 00.
With 5 No. 2½ Bottles.   Each, $8 25.

No. 149.

5 No. 3 Bottles.   Each, $7 00.

No. 148.

5 No. 2½ Bottles.   Each, $6 25.

No. 82.

5 No. 1 Bottles.   Each, $5 25.
With 5 No. 41 Bottles.   Each, $4 25.

No. 145.

With 5 No. 41 Bottles.   Each, $4 25.
With 4 No. 41 Bottles.   Each,   4 00.

No. 142.

5 No 41 Bottles.
Each, $4 25.

With 4 No. 41 Bottles.
Each, $4 00.

Bottles Furnished

At the Following Rates.

WITH PLATED MUSTARD AND PEPPER TOPS.

Nos. 41, 44 and 45,	$3 00 per dozen.
Nos. 3 1-2, 4 and 5,	4 75 per dozen.
No. 2 1-2,	5 25 per dozen.
Ground Cup Bottles,	6 60 per dozen.
Wreath Cup Bottles,	6 60 per dozen.

No. 147.

5 No. 41 Bottles.
Each, $4 00.

With 4 No. 41 Bottles.
Each, $3 75.

WINE STANDS
PLATED ON
NICKEL SILVER.

No. 081.
No. 81 Bottles.   Each, $54 50.

No. 080.
No. 81 Bottles.   Each, $53 25.

No. 088.
No. 88 Bottles.   Each, $36 50.

No. 04492.
White No. 92 Bottles and Glasses.
Grecian or Flower Engraved.   Each, $34 50.

Plated on White Metal.

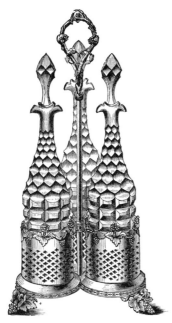

No. 10.

With Best White bottles.   Each, $24 00.

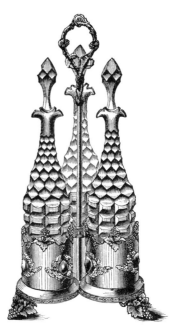

No. 20.

With Best White Bottles.   Each, $24 00.
No. 20 with Engine Frame.   Each, $24 00.
No. 20 with Grecian Chased Frame.   Each, $26 75.

No. 30.

With Best Colored Bottles and Wine Goblets to match.
Each, $40 00.
White Bottles and Goblets, or Gilt Goblets.   Each, $36 00.
With Gilt Chased Goblets.   Each, $42 00.

No. 40.

With Best White Bottles.   Each, $19 00.
With Best Colored Bottles.   Each,   22 00.
Chased or Engine, with Best Colored Bottles.   Each, $24 00.
Chased or Engine, with Best White Bottles.   Each,   22 00.

PITCHER WAITERS

PLATED ON

NICKEL SILVER.

No. 070.

Size, 16 inches, Fine Engraved and Cut Pitcher and Tumblers.

Each $44 00.

No. 060.

Size, 16 inches, Fine Engraved and Cut Pitcher and Tumblers.

Each, $40 00.

PITCHER WAITER

PLATED ON

WHITE METAL.

No. 30.

Each, $24 00.

PICKLE OR PRESERVE STANDS

PLATED ON

NICKEL SILVER.

No. 082.

No. 500 Bottles. Each. $26 50.
With No. 10 Bottles. Each, $22 50.

No 0709.

No. 500 Bottles. Each, $24 00.
With No. 10 Bottles. Each, $20 00.

No. 04480.

No. 12 Bottles. Each, $20 00.

No. 022.

No. 10 Bottles. Each, $18 50.

No. 021.

No. 10 Bottles. Each, $18 50.

No. 088.

Each, $15 00.

No. 04460.

Each, $18 00.

No. 04468.

Each, $16 50.

Bottles in No. 04460 and No. 04468 are not as represented in Cuts, but are Grecian or Flower Engraved.

EGG STANDS

PLATED ON
NICKEL SILVER.

No. 070.
With 4 Cups.   Each, $18 50.
With 6 Cups.   Each,   24 00.

No. 01981.
With 4 Cups and Spoons.   Each, $10 50.
With 3 Cups and Spoons.   Each,   7 75.

No. 70.
Same as No. 070 but plated on White Metal.
With 4 Cups.   Each, $12 50.
With 6 Cups.   Each,   15 25.

No. 060.

Each, $12 00.

Egg Stands

Plated on White Metal.

No. 50.
With 12 Gilt Cups and 12 Gilt Spoons.
Each, $30 00.

With Cups, Engine Turned.
Each, $34 50.

Custard or Ice Cream Stand

Plated on White Metal.

No. 1.
With 12 Gilt Spoons, and 12 Gilt Cups and Stand.
Each, $44 00.
With 12 Gilt Spoons, and 12 Gilt Cups and Stand,
Chased or Engine Turned.   Each, $50 00.

CAKE DISHES AND CAKE BASKETS

PLATED ON

NICKEL SILVER.

No. 060, Cake Basket.

10½ inches. Each, $24 50.

No. 060 1-2.

11½ inches. Each, 26 00.

No. 061, Cake Dish.

Each, $26 00.

No. 061, Cake Basket.

With Bail Handles same price.

No. 063, Cake Dish.

Each, $24 50.

No. 063, Cake Basket.

With Bail Handles same price.

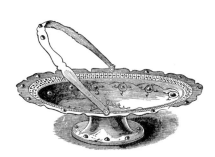

No. 08000.

Each, $14 00.

No. 07000.

Each, $18 00.

No 06000.

Each, $17 00.

No. 05000.

Each, $18 00.

No. 04000.

Each, $12 00.

No. 03000.

Each, $10 00.

CAKE BASKETS

WHITE METAL.

No. 1950.

Medallion and Chased.	Each,	$10 50.
X Medallion and Chased.	Each,	11 25.
XX Medallion and Chased.	Each,	12 00.
XX Chased.	Each,	12 00.
Engraved.	Each,	10 50.
Plain.	Each,	8 50.

No. 1866, XX Medallion or Chased.

XX Medallion.	Each,	$12 00.
X Medallion.	Each,	11 25.
Medallion.	Each,	10 50.
Engraved.	Each,	10 50.
Plain.	Each,	8 50.

No. 1696, Medallion Engraved.

Medallion Plain, 10½ inch. Each, $8 00.
Medallion and Engraved, 10½ inch. Each, $9 00.

* No. 1697.

Medallion Plain, 11½ inch. Each, $9 25.
Medallion and Engraved, 11½ inch. Each, 10 25.

No. 999.
Each, $10 00.

No. 888.
Each, $9 25.

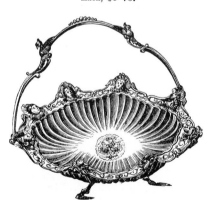

No. 777.
Each, $9 75.

† No. 666.
Each, $9 00.

† No. 555.
Each, $9 00.

No. 1812.
Each, $10 75.

No. 1813.
Gilt Inside. Each, $14 25.

* Same as No. 1696 only larger.   † These Baskets have a heavy Beaded Border instead of the one represented in Cut.

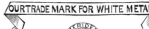

Plated on White Metal.

No. 1690, Engine.

Engine.	Each,	$9 25.
Medallion.	Each,	10 50.
X Medallion.	Each,	11 25.
XX Medallion.	Each,	12 00.
Plain.	Each,	8 50.

No. 1864.

Richly Embossed.   Each, $13 00.

No. 1919.

Each, $8 50.

Engine.   Each, $9 25.

No. 1677.
Each, $8 00.
Grecian Chased.   Each, $11 25.

No. 1675.

Each, $9 25.

No. 1588.
11 inch.   Each, $7 25.
No. 1589 same as No. 1588, only 12 inch.
Each, $8 00.

No. 1610.
Each, $7 75.

No. 1615.
Each, $7 50.

No. 1492.
Each, $10 50.

No. 1491.
Each, $10 00.

No. 1491, Engine.
Each, $10 50.

FRUIT STANDS

PLATED ON

WHITE METAL.

No. 1492.
Each, $14 00.

No. 1491.
Each, $12 50.

Berry or Preserve Dishes and Baskets

PLATED ON

NICKEL SILVER.

No. 01000.
Standard and Bottom plated on Nickel Silver.
With Oval or Round Glass Dishes, Assorted Colors.
Each, $28 00.

No. 01956.

Each, $10 00.

No. 01952.
With Plain Dish. Each, $14 00.
With Fine Ruby or Green Dish.
Each, $16 00.

Berry or Preserve Dishes and Baskets

PLATED ON

WHITE METAL.

No. 10, Open.
Each, $12 50.

No. 5, Open.
Each, $10 50.

All Goods bearing our Trade Marks
are Triple Plate.

Plated on White Metal.

No. 12.

White Ground Glass Lining.   Each, $14 00.

*No. 13.   Each, $13 25.
*No. 14.   Each, 12 75.
*No. 15.   Each, 12 00.

No. 1968.

Ruby Lining.   Each, $12 00.

No. 11.

Ruby Lining.   Each, $6 75.
White Lining.   Each, 6 00.

No. 1949.

With Ruby Glass Linings.   Each, $8 00.

No. 1965.

With Ruby Glass Linings.   Each, $8 50.
No. 1965 is now furnished with Chain.

No. 1967.

With Ruby Glass Linings.   Each, $11 00.

CELERY STANDS

Plated on Nickel Silver.   Plated on White Metal.

No. 0100.

Each, $20 00.

No. 1.
With White Glass.
Open.   Each, $9 25.
Grecian Chased.   Each, $10 00.
Medallion and Chased.   Each, 10 50.

·No. 5.

Plain.   Each, $12 00.

Chased or Medallion.   Each, $13 25.

*Nos. 13, 14 and 15 have same frame as No. 12 Cut above, but different Lining as is indicated by the price.

BUTTER DISHES

PLATED ON

WHITE METAL.

No. 82, Revolving, Plain.

Plain.	Each,	$6 75.
Engine.	Each,	7 50.
Medallion.	Each,	8 25.
Engraved.	Each,	8 25.
Chased.	Each,	8 25.

No. 1866, Revolving, same as No. 82, only has feet and trimmings to match No. 1866 Tea Set.

No. 82, Revolving, Engine.

(With Hooks for Knife.)

No. 81, Revolving.

(With Hooks for Knife.)

Plain.	Each,	$6 75.
Engine.	Each,	7 50.
Damask Chased.	Each,	8 25.
Grecian Chased.	Each,	8 25.
Medallion,	Each,	8 25.

No. 5000, Revolving.

(With Hooks for Knife.)

Engine.   Each, $10 00.

Grecian Chased. Each, 11 00.

No. 83, Oval, Revolving.

Plain.	Each,	$8 00.
Engine.	Each,	8 75.
Grecian.	Each,	9 75.
Medallion.	Each,	9 75.
Engraved.	Each,	9 75.

† No. 1867, Oval, Revolving.

(To match No. 1867 Tea Set.)

Plain.	Each,	$8 00.
Engine.	Each,	8 75.
Grecian.	Each,	9 75.
Medallion.	Each,	9 75.
Engraved.	Each,	9 75.

No. 3700, Chased.

Chased, with Gilt Strainer.
     Each, $9 25.
Engine, with Gilt Strainer.
     Each, $8 50.

No. 4000, Chased.

Grecian Chased.	Each,	$8 50.
Damask Chased.	Each,	8 25.
Engine.	Each,	8 00.
Plain.	Each,	6 75.

No. 1000.

Plain.	Each,	$5 25.
Engine.	Each,	6 00.
Chased.	Each,	6 75.

No. 1165.

Plain.	Each,	$6 25.
Engine.	Each,	7 00.
Damask Chased.	Each,	7 50.
Grecian Chased.	Each,	8 00.

† No. 1868 Butter Dish same pattern as No. 1867, except with trimmings to match No. 1868 Tea Set.

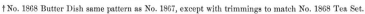

82

SYRUP CUPS AND PLATES

PLATED ON

WHITE METAL.

No. 99, Engine Turned.

Plain, without Plate.	Each, $5 00.
Engine, without Plate.	Each, 5 50.
Damask Chased, without Plate.	Each, 6 00
Grecian Chased, without Plate.	Each, 6 50.
Plain, with Plate.	Each, 6 50.
Engine, with Plate.	Each, 7 00.
Damask Chased, with Plate.	Each, 7 50.
Grecian Chased, with Plate.	Each, 8 00.

No. 98, Engine Turned.

Plain, without Plate.	Each, $4 00.
Engine, without Plate.	Each, 4 50.
Damask Chased, without Plate.	Each, 5 00.
Grecian Chased, without Plate.	Each, 5 50.
Plain, with Plate.	Each, 5 25.
Engine, with Plate.	Each, 5 75.
Damask Chased, with Plate	Each, 6 25.
Grecian Chased, with Plate.	Each, 6 75.

No. 97, Engine Turned.

Plain, without Plate.	Each, $3 50.
Engine, without Plate.	Each, 4 00.
Damask Chased, without Plate.	Each, 4 25.
Grecian Chased, without Plate.	Each, 4 75.
Plain, with Plate.	Each, 4 50.
Engine, with Plate.	Each, 5 00.
Damask Chased, with Plate.	Each, 5 25.
Grecian Chased, with Plate.	Each, 5 75.

No. 96, Engine Turned.

Plain, without Plate.	Each, $5 25.
Engine, without Plate.	Each, 6 00.
Damask Chased, without Plate.	Each, 6 25.
Grecian Chased, without Plate.	Each, 6 75.
Plain, with Plate.	Each, 7 00.
Engine, with Plate.	Each, 7 75.
Damask Chased, with Plate.	Each, 8 00.
Grecian Chased, with Plate.	Each, 8 25.

No. 95, Chased.   **No. 90, Grecian Chased.**   **No. 90, Chased.**

Plain, without Plate.	Each, $4 00.
Engine, without Plate.	Each, 4 50.
Damask Chased, without Plate.	Each, 5 00
Grecian Chased, without Plate.	Each, 5 50.
Plain, with Plate.	Each, 5 25.
Engine, with Plate.	Each, 5 75.
Damask Chased, with Plate.	Each, 6 25.
Grecian Chased, with Plate.	Each, 6 75.

Plain, without Plate.	Each, $3 50.
Engine, without Plate.	Each, 4 00.
Damask Chased, without Plate.	Each, 4 25.
Grecian Chased, without Plate.	Each, 4 75.
Plain, with Plate.	Each, 4 50.
Engine, with Plate.	Each, 5 00.
Damask Chased, with Plate.	Each, 5 25.
Grecian Chased, with Plate.	Each, 5 75.

GOBLETS AND CUPS

PLATED ON

NICKEL SILVER.

No. 01396, Engine Turned.
Plain Plated.　　Each, $4 00.
Plain Gilt.　　Each, 5 00.
Engine Plated.　Each, 5 00.
Engine Gilt.　　Each, 6 00.
Grecian or Damask Chased Plated.
Each, $5 00.
Grecian or Damask Chased Gilt.
Each, $6 00.

No. 01395, Engine Turned.
Plain Plated.　　Each, $2 25.
Plain Gilt.　　Each, 3 25.
Engine Plated.　Each, 3 00.
Engine Gilt.　　Each, 4 00.
Grecian or Damask Chased Plated.
Each, $3 00.
Grecian or Damask Chased Gilt.
Each, $4 00.

No. 016.
Plain Plated.　　Each, $3 25.
Plain Gilt.　　Each, 4 25.
Engine Plated.　Each, 4 25.
Engine Gilt.　　Each, 5 25.
Grecian or Damask Chased Plated.
Each, $4 25.
Grecian or Damask Chased Gilt.
Each, $5 25.

No. 01375, Engine Turned.
Plain Plated.　　Each, $3 75.
Plain Gilt.　　Each, 4 50.
Engine Plated.　Each, 4 50.
Engine Gilt.　　Each, 5 25.
Grecian or Damask Chased Plated.
Each, $4 50.
Grecian or Damask Chased Gilt.
Each, $5 25.

No. 01373, Engine Turned.
Plain Plated.　　Each, $3 00.
Plain Gilt.　　Each, 3 75.
Engine Plated.　Each, 4 00.
Engine Gilt.　　Each, 4 50.
Grecian or Damask Chased Plated.
Each, $4 00.
Grecian or Damask Chased Gilt.
Each, $4 50.

No. 03.
Plain Plated.　　Each, $4 00.
Plain Gilt.　　Each, 5 00.
Engine Plated.　Each, 5 00.
Engine Gilt.　　Each, 6 00.
Grecian or Damask Chased Plated.
Each, $5 00.
Grecian or Damask Chased Gilt.
Each, $6 00.

No. 021.
Plain.　　Each, $3 75.
Plain Gilt.　　Each, 4 25.
Grecian or Damask Chased Plated.
Each, $4 50.
Grecian or Damask Chased Gilt.
Each, $5 25.

No. 04.
Plain Plated.　Each, $4 50.
Plain Gilt.　　Each, 5 25.
Engine or Grecian Chased Plated.
Each, $5 50.
Engine or Grecian Chased Gilt.
Each, $6 25.

No. 05, Tumbler.

Each, $4 25.

No. 013.

No. 011.

No.	Plain Plated.	Plain Gilt.	Engraved Plated.	Engraved Gilt.
011.	$3 75	$4 25	$4 50	$5 00
*012.	4 50	5 00	5 50	6 00
013.	5 25	5 75	6 50	7 00

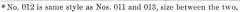

*No. 012 is same style as Nos. 011 and 013, size between the two.

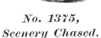

Plated on White Metal.

No. 1375,
Scenery Chased.

No. 1375,
Plain.

No. 1374,
Medallion.

No. 1374,
Engine.

No. 1374,
Plain.

Plain Plated.	Each, $2 25.
Plain Gilt.	Each, 3 00.
Engine Plated.	Each, 2 50.
Engine Gilt.	Each, 3 25.
Grecian or Damask Chased Plated.	Each, $3 00.
Grecian or Damask Chased Gilt.	Each, 3 75.
Scenery Gilt.	Each, $5 25.

Plain Plated.	Each, $2 00.
Plain Gilt.	Each, 2 75.
Engine Plated.	Each, 2 25.
Engine Gilt.	Each, 3 00.
Grecian or Damask Chased Plated.	Each, $2 50.
Grecian or Damask Chased Gilt.	Each, 3 25.
Medallion Plated.	Each, 2 50.
Medallion Gilt.	Each, 3 25.

No. 1373,
Plain.

No. 1373,
Engine.

No. 1371,
Engraved.

No. 1370.
Grecian Chased.

No. 1370,
Engine.

No. 1370,
Plain.

Plain Plated.	Each, $1 75.
Plain Gilt.	Each, 2 50.
Engine Plated.	Each, 2 00.
Engine Gilt.	Each, 2 75.
Grecian or Damask Chased Plated.	Each, $2 50.
Grecian or Damask Chased Gilt.	Each, $3 25.

Plain Plated.	Each, $1 60.
Plain Gilt.	Each, 2 25.
Engraved Plated.	Each, 2 25.
Engraved Gilt.	Each, 3 00.

Plain Plated.	Each, $1 65.
Plain Gilt.	Each, 2 25.
Engine Plated.	Each, 2 00.
Engine Gilt.	Each, 2 60.
Grecian or Damask Chased Plated.	Each, $2 25.
Grecian or Damask Chased Gilt.	Each, 3 00.

No. 33,
Chased.

No. 36,
Plain.

No. 33,
Plain.

No. 34,
Wreath Chased.

No. 34,
Grecian Chased.

No. 34,
Medallion.

No. 37,
Engraved.

No. 39,
Engraved.

No.	Plain Plated.	Plain Gilt.	Engine Plated.	Engine Gilt.	Grecian or Damask Chased Plated.	Grecian or Damask Chased Gilt.	Medallion Plated.	Medallion Gilt.
33	$1 75	$2 25	$2 00	$2 50	$2 25	$2 75	$2 25	$2 75
34	1 65	2 15	1 90	2 40	2 15	2 65	2 15	2 65
36	2 00	2 50	2 25	2 75	2 50	3 00	2 50	3 00
37	1 75	2 25	2 00	2 50	2 25	2 75	2 25	2 75
*38	1 90	2 40	2 15	2 65	2 40	2 90	2 40	2 90
39	2 25	2 75	2 50	3 00	2 75	3 25	2 75	3 25

*No. 38 in size is between Nos. 37 and 39, but same style.

SPOON HOLDERS

PLATED ON
NICKEL SILVER.

No. 019, Plain.		No. 01396, Engine Turned.		No. 050, Chased.	
Plain Plated.	Each, $5 25.	Plain Plated.	Each, $4 25.	Plain Plated.	Each, $4 75.
Plain Gilt.	Each, 6 25.	Plain Gilt.	Each, 5 25.	Plain Gilt.	Each, 5 75.
Engine Plated.	Each, 6 00	Engine Plated.	Each, 5 25.	Engine Plated.	Each, 6 00.
Engine Gilt.	Each, 7 00.	Engine Gilt.	Each, 6 25.	Engine Gilt.	Each, 7 00.
Grecian Chased Plated.	Each, 7 00.	Grecian Chased Plated.	Each, 6 25.	Chased Plated.	Each, 6 25.
Grecian Chased Gilt.	Each, 8 00.	Grecian Chased Gilt.	Each, 7 25.	Chased Gilt.	Each, 7 25.

SPOON HOLDERS

PLATED ON
WHITE METAL.

No. 1866, Engine. No. 1866, Silver Engraved.   No. 1866, Medallion.   No. 1860, Grecian Chased.

Plain Plated.	Each,	$4 00.	Plain Plated.	Each, $3 75.
Plain Gilt.	Each,	4 75.	Plain Gilt.	Each, 4 50.
Engine Plated.	Each,	4 25.	Engine Plated.	Each, 4 00.
Engine Gilt.	Each,	5 00.	Engine Gilt.	Each, 4 75.
Silver Engraved Plated.	Each,	5 25.	Damask Chased Plated.	Each, 4 75.
Silver Engraved Gilt.	Each,	6 00.	Damask Chased Gilt.	Each, 5 50.
Grecian Chased Plated.	Each,	5 25.	Grecian Chased Plated.	Each, 5 00.
Grecian Chased Gilt.	Each,	6 00.	Grecian Chased Gilt.	Each, 5 75.
Medallion Plated.	Each,	5 25.		
Medallion Gilt.	Each,	6 00.		

No. 460, Wreath Chased.		No. 1380, Wreath Chased.		No. 1380, Engine Turned.	
Plain Plated.	Each, $3 25.	Plain Plated.	Each, $3 00.		
Plain Gilt.	Each, 4 00.	Plain Gilt.	Each, 3 75.		
Engine Plated.	Each, 3 75.	Engine Plated.	Each, 3 25.		
Engine Gilt.	Each, 4 50.	Engine Gilt.	Each, 4 00.		
Grecian Chased Plated.	Each, $4 25.	Grecian Chased Plated.	Each, 4 00.		
Grecian Chased Gilt.	Each, 5 00.	Grecian Chased Gilt.	Each, 4 75.		
Damask or Wreath Chased Plated.	Each, 4 00.				
Damask or Wreath Chased Gilt.	Each, 4 75.				

TOAST RACKS

PLATED ON

NICKEL SILVER.

No. 03.

Each, $9 25.

No. 04.

Each, $7 25.

No. 07.

Each, $11 25.

No. 08.

Each, $11 25.

No. 09.

Each, $11 25.

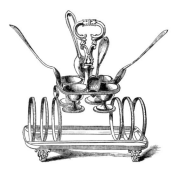

No. 010.

Each, $16 00.

TOAST RACK

PLATED ON

WHITE METAL.

No. 10.

Each, $5 00.

87

CALL BELLS

PLATED ON

BELL METAL.

No. 100.	No. 200.	No. 300.	No. 500.	No. 1100.	No. 1200.
Per dozen, $10 50.	Per dozen, $10 50.	Marbleized Iron Base.	Per dozen, $13 00.	White Marble Base.	Per Dozen, $13 50.
		Per dozen, $12 50.		Per dozen, $13 50.	

HAND BELLS

PLATED ON

BELL METAL.

No. 050.	No. 060.	No. 070.	No. 080.	No. 085.
Per dozen, $7 50.	Per dozen, $7 00.	Per dozen, $5 50.	Per dozen, $7 50.	Per dozen, $18 00.

PATENT CALL BELLS

PLATED ON

BELL METAL.

No. 1300.	No. 1400.	No. 1500.	No. 1600.	No. 1700.
Per dozen, $18 00.	Black Base. Per dozen, $17 00.	Per dozen, $15 00.	Per dozen, $17 00.	Per dozen, $18 00.

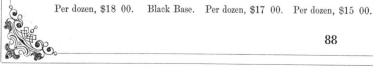

NAPKIN RINGS

PLATED ON

NICKEL SILVER.

No. 0200.	No. 0300.	No. 035.	No. 030.
Medallion Engraved. Per dozen, $14 00.	Engraved Medallion. Per dozen, $16 00.	Per dozen, $10 50.	Plain. Per dozen, $10 50.
Plain Medallion. Per dozen, 10 00.	Plain Medallion. Per dozen, 12 00.		Engine. Per dozen, 14 00.

No. 020.	No. 025.	No. 026.
Plain. Per dozen, $8 50.	Plain. Per dozen, $8 00.	Grecian. Per dozen, $8 00.
Engine. Per dozen, 12 00.	Engine. Per dozen, 11 50.	

NAPKIN RINGS

PLATED ON

WHITE METAL.

No. 10, Plain.	No. 45, Engine.	No. 40, Engine.	No. 40, Grecian.
Plain. Per dozen, $4 00.	Plain. Per dozen, $5 00.	Plain. Per dozen, $4 50.	Per dozen, $4 50.
Engine. Per dozen, 6 00.	Engine. Per dozen, 7 25.	Engine. Per dozen, 7 00.	Per dozen, 7 00.
	Grecian. Per dozen, 8 00.	Grecian. Per dozen, 7 75.	Per dozen, 7 75.

No. 60, Engine.	No. 60, Grecian.	No. 50, Engine.	No. 80, Engine.
Plain.	Per dozen, $5 25.	Plain. Per dozen, $5 25.	Plain. Per dozen, $5 00.
Engine.	Per dozen, 7 50.	Engine. Per dozen,' 7 75.	Engine. Per dozen, 7 50.
Grecian.	Per dozen, 8 25.		

No. 90.
Engine. Per dozen, $4 00.

PLATED

KNIFE RESTS.

No. 1.	No. 2.	No. 5, Six Sided Bar.
Per dozen, $8 00.	Per dozen, $8 00.	Per dozen, $10 50.

S A L T S

PLATED ON

N I C K E L   S I L V E R.

No. 010.

Gilt.   Per pair, $5 00.

*No. 02, Gilt.   Per pair, $4 00.

No. 020, Individual Salts.

Gilt, with Case.   Per dozen, $14 00.

No. 08.

Plain Gilt.   Per pair, $8 00.

Chased Gilt.   Per pair, 9 25.

S A L T S

PLATED ON

W H I T E   M E T A L.

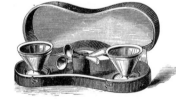

No. 18, Gilt.

Plain Gilt.   Per pair, $4 25.

Engine Gilt.   Per pair, 4 75.

With Case and Spoons.

Plain Gilt.   Per pair, $6 25.

Engine Gilt.   Per pair, 6 75.

No. 22, Gilt.

Plain Gilt.   Per pair, $4 25.

With Case and Spoons.

Plain Gilt.   Per pair, $6 50.

† With No. 30 Medallion Gilt Mustard.   Per case, $12 50.

No. 16, Gilt Engine.

Per pair, $3 50.

No. 15, Gilt Engine.

Per pair, $3 75.

No. 1859, Gilt Engine.

Per pair, $3 25.

No. 1835, Gilt Engine.

Per pair, $3 75.

No. 19.

With Ruby Glass Lining.

Per pair, $4 50.

No. 21.

With Ruby Glass Lining.

Per pair, $5 00.

*Same as No. 010 only smaller.

†For Cut of No. 30 Mustard, see page 109.

MUSTARD CUPS

PLATED ON

WHITE METAL.

No. 30, Gilt.   **No. 12.**

Engraved or Medallion.   Each, $4 75.   Glass Lining.   Each, $4 00.

Plain.   Each, $4 25.

PEPPER BOXES

PLATED ON

NICKEL SILVER.

No. 01.   **No. 02.**

Plain Silver Pattern.   Each, $5 00.   Engraved.   Each, $6 25.

Chased Silver Pattern.   Each, 6 25.   Plain.   Each, 5 25.

No. 3.

Same as No. 02, Plated on White Metal.

Engraved.   Each, $3 00.

Plain.   Each, 2 75.

SARDINE BOX

PLATED ON

WHITE METAL.

No. 1867.

Plain.   Each, $5 00.
Engraved.   Each, 6 00.
Medallion.   Each, 6 50.

Porcupine

Tooth Pick Holder.

SUGAR SIFTER

PLATED ON

WHITE METAL.

No. 20.

Plain.   Each, $3 25.
Engraved.   Each, 3 75.

Each, $1 50.

Gilt.   Each, $2 00.

TOILET SETS.

FRAMES PLATED ON

WHITE METAL.

No. 1, Antique.
1 Bottle Cologne.   Each, $5 00.

No. 2, Antique.
2 Bottles Cologne.   Each, $10 50.

No. 3, Antique.
2 Bottles and Puff Box.   Each, $15 00.

Puff Boxes, with Puff included.
Each, $2 25.

CANDLESTICKS

PLATED ON

WHITE METAL.

| ***No. 9.*** | ***No. 10.*** | ***No. 11.*** | ***No. 105.*** | ***No. 104.*** | ***No. 103.*** | ***No. 102.*** |
| Per pair, $11 00. | Per pair, $10 00. | Per pair, $9 25. | Per pair, $6 00. | Per pair, $5 25. | Per pair, $5 00. | Per pair, $4 75. |

Plated on White Metal.

No. 8.
Per pair, $8 00.

No. 5.
Per pair, $5 75.

No. 4.
Per pair, $5 25.

No. 3.
Per pair, $5 00.

No. 2.
Per pair, $4 50.

No. 45.
Per pair, $4 25.

No. 55.
Per pair, $5 75.

No. 93.
With Extinguisher.
Per pair, $6 00.
With Extinguisher and Snuffer.
Per pair, $7 00.

No. 92.
With Extinguisher.
Per pair, $5 00.
Without Extinguisher.
Per pair, $4 50.

No. 90.
Per pair, $5 75.

No. 91.
With Extinguisher.
Per pair, $5 25.

No. 91.
Per pair, $4 75.

FIREMEN'S TRUMPETS
PLATED ON
NICKEL SILVER.

Extra Fine.

Plain.   Each, $40 00.

Chased or Engraved.   Each, 46 75.

Medallion or X Chased or Engraved.   Each, $50 75.

Medallion or XX Chased or Engraved.   Each, 54 75.

Gilt, $4 50 extra.

COMMUNION SETS.

CONSISTING OF

One Flagon, two Goblets, two Plates and one Baptismal Bowl.

PLATED ON

WHITE METAL.

No. 12.

		Plated.	White Metal Unplated.
No. 12.	Flagon, 2 quarts, Round Beaded Mount,	$10 50.	$5 25.
*No. 11.	Flagon, 1 quart, Round Beaded Mount,	9 25.	4 50.
No. 12.	Goblet, large, . . .	3 25.	1 75.
No. 12.	Plates, 10 inch, . . .	4 00.	1 75.
No. 12.	Paten, ...	6 75.	2 75.
No. 12.	Baptismal Bowl, . . .	7 25.	3 00.

No. 14, same as No. 12, with different style Beading and same price.

No. 10.   No. 10.   No. 10.   No. 10.

		Plated.	White Metal Unplated.
No. 10.	Flagon, 2 quarts, ...	$10 50.	$5 25
†No. 9.	Flagon, 1 quart, ...	9 25.	4 75.
No. 10.	Goblet, medium size, . . .	4 00.	2 00.
No. 10.	Plate, 10 inch, ...	4 00.	2 00.
No. 10.	Paten, ...	6 75.	2 75.
No. 10.	Baptismal Bowl, . . .	7 25.	3 00.

In Sets of Six Pieces.

Consisting of Flagon, Baptismal Bowl, two Goblets and two Plates.

		In Metal.	Plated.
No. 14.	. . . . .	$15 25.	$32 25.
No. 12.	. . . . .	15 25.	32 25.
No. 11.	. . . . .	14 50.	31 00.
No. 10.	. . . . .	16 25.	34 75.
No. 9.	. . . . .	15 50.	33 50.

Patens extra at prices quoted above.

* Same style as No. 12.   † Same style as No. 10.

Plated on First Quality Nickel Silver.

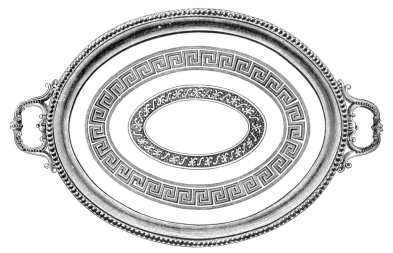

No. 5010, Chased.   **No. 5010, Chased.**

10 inches.	Each, $10 00.
12 inches.	Each, 14 50.
14 inches.	Each, 19 50.
16 inches.	Each, 24 50.
18 inches.	Each, 32 50.
20 inches.	Each, 46 50.
22 inches.	Each, 58 00.
24 inches.	Each, 69 00.
26 inches.	Each, 83 00.
28 inches.	Each, 98 75.
30 inches.	Each, 114 50.

No. 5011, Chased.

10 inches.	Each, $12 00.
12 inches.	Each, 17 50.
14 inches.	Each, 23 50.
16 inches.	Each, 29 50.
18 inches.	Each, 38 50.

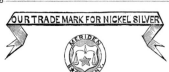

Plated on First Quality Nickel Silver.

No. 1, 26 Inches, Scenery.

No. 1, 16 Inches, Scroll Pattern.

No. 1, 10 Inches, Scroll Pattern.

Scroll and Acorn Pattern, Engraved or Chased.

10 inches.	Each, $14 50.
12 inches.	Each, 19 50.
14 inches.	Each, 26 50.
16 inches.	Each, 32 00.
18 inches.	Each, 40 50.
20 inches.	Each, 56 50.
22 inches.	Each, 73 00.
24 inches.	Each, 83 00.
26 inches.	Each, 100 00.
28 inches.	Each, 114 00.
30 inches.	Each, 126 50.

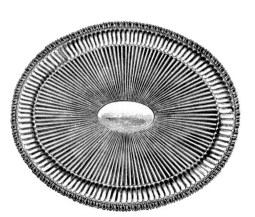

16 Inches, Fluted, on Feet.

12 inches. Each, $10 25.
16 inches. Each, 15 00.

WAITERS

PLATED ON

WHITE METAL.

No. 3, Engine Turned.

No. 4, Medallion Chased.

	Engine.	Medallion or Grecian Chased.
10 inches.	$5 50.	$6 75.
12 inches.	7 00.	8 75.
14 inches.	9 75.	11 50.
16 inches.	11 50.	14 00.
18 inches.	13 00.	17 00.

	Engine.	Medallion or Grecian Chased.
20 inches.	$18 00.	$24 00.
With Handles, 22 inches.	24 00.	33 00.
24 inches.	28 00.	37 50.
26 inches.	32 00.	44 00.

No. 5, Oblong Waiter, Chased.

	Chased.	X Extra Fine Chased.
12 inches.	$8 75.	$9 50.
14 inches.	11 50.	12 50.
16 inches.	14 00.	15 00.

ENTREE DISHES

WITH

Lock Handle, Hot Water Dish, Frame and Lamp complete.

PLATED ON

NICKEL SILVER.

No. 04410. Eleven Inch.

No. 04400. Twelve Inch.

No.	Inches.	Plain, Without Hot Water Dish.	Chased, Without Hot Water Dish.	Plain, With Hot Water Dish.	Chased, With Hot Water Dish.
4410	11	$50 00	$56 00	$62 00	$68 25
4410	12	54 50	61 00	66 50	73 25
4400	11	50 00	56 00	62 00	68 25
4400	12	54 50	61 00	66 50	73 25

No. 041. One Pint Gravy Boat.

Plain Plated.   Each, $11 75.
Plain Gilded.   Each, 13 50.

***No. 040. Half Pint Gravy Boat.**

Plain Plated.   Each, $15 50.
Plain Gilded.   Each, 17 50.

* Same in appearance as No. 041, only smaller.

No. 01, Beef Steak Dish.

Plain.   Each, $22 25.

TUREENS

WHITE METAL.

No. 1837, Grecian Chased. Three Quarts.

Style.	1½ Pints.	1 Quart.	1½ Quarts.	2 Quarts.	3 Quarts.
Plain,	$8 50	$9 25	$10 50	$12 50	$14 50
Grecian Chased,	11 25	12 00	14 00	16 50	18 50

No. 1835, Oyster. Three Quarts.

No. 1835, Soup. Four Quarts.

Style.	3 Quarts.	4 Quarts.	8 Quarts.	16 Quarts.
Plain,	$13 25	$18 00	$32 00	$53 00
Plain and Waiter,	17 50	22 25	36 25	57 25
Engine,	14 50	19 25	34 50	58 00
Engine and Plain Waiter,	18 75	23 50	38 75	62 25
Grecian Chased,	18 50	23 25	40 00	66 50
Grecian Chased and Plain Waiter,	22 75	27 50	44 25	70 75

No. 1941, Medallion, Chased Soup. Four Quarts.

No. 1941, Grecian Chased Soup. Six Quarts.

No. 1799, Gravy.

	3 Quarts.	4 Quarts.	6 Quarts.
Plain,	$15 75.	$19 00.	$25 00.
Medallion,	21 00.	25 00.	32 25.
Grecian Chased,	21 00.	25 00.	32 25.

Plain. Each, $5 50.

COCOANUT SHAPED DIPPERS

PLATED ON

WHITE METAL.

WITH WOOD HANDLES.

No. 1, Plain.

Plain Plated.   Each, $2 00.
Plain Gilt.   Each, 2 50.

No 1, Engine.

Engine Plated.   Each, $2 50.
Engine Gilt.   Each, 3 00.

No. 1, Chased.

Chased Plated.   Each, $3 00.
Chased Gilt.   Each, 3 50.

EGG BOILERS

PLATED ON

WHITE METAL.

No. 1.

Plain.   Each, $14 00.
Engine.   Each, 15 25.
Grecian or Damask Chased.   Each, $16 25.

No. 2.

Plain.   Each, $10 00.
Engine.   Each, 11 00.
Grecian or Damask Chased.   Each, $12 00.

BAR FIXTURES

SUGAR OR CRACKER BOWLS.

No. 8, Plain Medallion.

Plated on White Metal.

Medallion not Plated.   Each, $6 50.
Medallion Plated.   Each, 12 50.
Medallion Chased or Engraved Plated.   Each, $14 50.

*No. 7, Medallion.

Not Plated.   Each, $9 25.
Plated.   Each,   15 25.
Plated Chased or Engraved.   Each, $18 00.

*No. 6, Medallion.

Not Plated.   Each, $12 00.
Plated.   Each,   18 50.
Plated and Chased or Engraved.   Each, $21 25.

No. 15, Cut Glass.

Cover Plated on White Metal.

Each, $17 25.

No. 05, Engine Turned.

Plated on Nickel Silver.

Engine.   Each, $21 00.

Plain.   Each,   18 50.

TOBACCO BOXES.

No. 10, Engine Turned.

Plated on White Metal.

Each, $8 00.

PUNCH MUGS.

No. 01.
Plated on Nickel Silver.
Each, $9 25.

No. 02.
Plated on Nickel Silver.
Each, $10 50.

No. 10.
Plated on White Metal.
Each, $3 50.

*Same as No. 8 but larger, No. 6 being the largest of the three.

Bar Fixtures. (Continued.)

LIQUOR MIXERS.

No. 01, Engine.
Plated on Nickel Silver.

No. 01, Plain.　Each, $3 25.
No. 02, Plain.　Each,　3 00.
No. 01, Engine.　Each,　4 00.
No. 02, Engine.　Each,　3 50.

No. 3.　**No. 4.**
Plated on White Metal.

No. 3, Plain.　Each, $2 50.
No. 4, Plain.　Each,　2 25.
No. 3, Engine.　Each,　3 00.
No. 4, Engine.　Each,　2 75.

SODA TUMBLER HOLDER.

No. 1.
Plated on White Metal.
Plain.　Each, $2 25.
Engine.　Each,　2 75.

STRAINERS.

No. 01.
In Nickel Silver.　Each, $2 00.
Plated on Nickel Silver.　Each, $3 00.

TODDY STRAINER.

Plated on Albata.
Plain.　Per dozen, $8 00.
Olive.　Per dozen, 10 00.

CIGAR ASH HOLDER.

Plated on Nickel Silver.
Each, $4 50.

DECANTER STOPPLES

Hinge.　**Single Slide.**　**Double Slide.**
Quart.　Quart.　Quart.
Per dozen, $5 25.　Per dozen, $5 25.　Per dozen, $5 25.

"Williams'" Patent.
No. 1.　Per dozen, $5 25.
No. 2.　Per dozen,　5 25.
No. 3.　Per dozen,　5 25.

PATENT
BEER PITCHER.

Plated on White Metal.
Plain.　Each, $10 00.

CIGAR LAMPS.

No. 45.
Plated on White Metal.
Each, $5 00.

WASH BOWL AND PITCHER

PLATED ON

WHITE METAL.

Plain.　Each, $24 00.
Engine.　Each, 30 00.

Parlor Spittoons,

WITH

Lock Cover.

PLATED ON

WHITE METAL.

No. 1.
Plain.　Each, $4 50.
Engine.　Each, 5 25.
Grecian.　Each, 6 25.

Tooth Brush Dish

PLATED ON

WHITE METAL.

Each, $7 00.

SOAP DISH

PLATED ON

WHITE METAL.

Each, $6 00.

TOOTH BRUSH HOLDERS

PLATED ON

WHITE METAL.

Put up in Boxes of one-half dozen.
Per dozen, $7 25.
Unplated.　Per dozen, $4 50.

PATENT TOBACCO BOXES

PLATED ON

NICKEL SILVER.

No. 310.

Silver Plated, Fancy Top, O. G. Bottom, assorted in each half dozen.   Per dozen, $12 00.

No. 309, Plain.

Silver Plated, O. G. Shield.   Per dozen, $10 65.

DERBY SILVER CO., 1883

While no other company equaled or even approached Meriden Britannia in the number or variety of items produced, the demand for silverplate was so great in the 1860's and '70's that several other Connecticut companies were founded to cater to it. Prominent among them in the manufacture of holloware were the Wilcox Silverplate Co., founded (as Wilcox Britannia Co.) in 1865, the Middletown Plate Co., founded in 1864, the Meriden Silver Plate Co., founded in 1869, and the Derby Silver Co., founded in 1873. The latter was based in an industrial suburb of Derby, Conn., known as Birmingham, presumably as a compliment to the English silver center of the same name. Derby Silver Co. was in the original group that formed International Silver Co. in 1898.

Derby's designers may have lacked something of the suavity and sophistication of those employed at Meriden, but the quality of the company's workmanship and plating was high. The designs shown for 1883 reflect the latest styles of the decade. Shapes tend to be somewhat squat and high-shouldered, with high flaring handles. The craze for oriental motifs is evident. Pieces are liberally sprinkled with bamboo, chrysanthemums, goldfish, cranes and the like.

New finishes are also evident. A favorite was "satin bright out" in which the main surfaces of the piece were given a frosted matte finish, with the hand engraved decoration highly polished. Gilding, gold linings, and gold niello were used frequently.

Silverplate was obviously being used with a far more lavish hand. Tea sets were larger and involved more pieces; most standard sets included three pots (for coffee, tea and hot water) and almost all could be had with matching urn, butter dish, syrup cup and spoon holder. The individual ice water pitcher was virtually ignored. Far more attention was devoted to sets which included a tray, slop bowl and goblets or, in another version, the pitcher mounted on an elaborate stand in which it could be tilted with ease.

Many matching pieces could be ordered. A design featuring a small girl and a kitten was offered in an ice pitcher set, a waiter, and a child's plate. Old favorites such as casters remained in vogue, but more stress was placed on such items as toilet sets, vases, card receivers, elaborate fruit stands and epergnes. Many of these featured lavishly decorated glass inserts.

About half the plates showing holloware from Derby's 1883 catalog are reproduced in the following pages. Among the items also offered, but not reproduced, were six more tea sets, 12 cups, a communion set, four wine coolers, 20 call and hand bells, 32 caster sets, six peppers and vinegars, 28 separate cream jugs, sugars and syrup cups, two spoon holders, 10 cake baskets, nine butter dishes, a salad bowl, a dessert set, three tureens, two pudding dishes, two statuettes (like the bases of the epergnes shown on pages 146 and 154), two additional epergnes, seven jewel caskets, nine goblets, 13 berry dishes, four fruit stands, 10 napkin rings, 12 vases, four toilet sets, 13 pickle casters, nine ice water pitchers, 12 ice water pitchers sets, and another dozen trays and waiters.

Sizes for many of the pieces were indicated. Since the following facsimile has been reduced by about one-half, these are no longer accurate. Thus a piece described as one-third the size of the original is shown here one-sixth the actual size. The sometimes strange sounding words listed in parenthesis after the price of each item refer to the telegraphic ordering code described on page 108. All prices, of course, are those at which the items were sold in 1883.

DERBY SILVER CO'S

Illustrated Catalogue and Price List

OF

Electro Gold and Silver Plated

HOLLOW WARE,

Spoons, Knives, Forks, Etc.,

ON HARD WHITE METAL AND NICKEL SILVER.

STANDARD GOODS.

SALESROOMS: New York City, and Chicago, Ill.

FACTORIES: Birmingham, Conn., U. S. A.
Where all Communications should be addressed.

1883.

We take pleasure in presenting this Illustrated Catalogue of a portion of our Standard Manufactures.

The celebrity our wares have obtained during our many years experience has created a large demand for them, and we trust the issuing of these new and artistic patterns will meet the wants long felt by our patrons.

Constantly improving our Goods, adding new and improved machinery, and employing the most skillful artisans, our productions have attained an unrivaled reputation for Quality, Durability, Finish and Design.

Our manufacturing facilities, which have been more than doubled during the past two years, are now unsurpassed.

In the manufacture of "White Metal" and "Nickel Silver" Electro Plate, the first consideration is the base, or metal on which the Gold or Silver is deposited. Making these metals under our own supervision, at our works, we claim their superiority, believing that they are HARDER and WHITER than those commonly used, and therefore more durable, and capable of receiving a higher finish. The only assurance of sufficient plate on this line of wares is the integrity of the manufacturer. Maintaining the same High Standard in manufacturing in the future as in the past, our constant endeavor will be to produce goods which will be an honor to the trade and a credit to us as manufacturers.

DERBY SILVER COMPANY.

TELEGRAPHIC CODE.

EXPLANATION.

For Convenience and Economy in sending Telegraphic Orders, we have adopted a system by which various words represent our Goods, and in this Catalogue you will find with each piece a single word, *in parenthesis*, to be used as above.

In Telegraphing, great care should be taken in the use of the right words, correctly spelled, etc.

By this system Telegraph Messages will be found very inexpensive. Night Messages will reduce the cost one-half.

EXAMPLE—Express zest waft weather weigh whiz wrinkle vine unlace thought.

This would read literally: Express one each, Number sixteen hundred and one Chased A Tea Set; Sixteen hundred and six Chased Swing Kettle; Six hundred and four fourteen inch Egyptian Chased Waiter; Naught two thousand nine and a half Tilting Pitcher Set, P. L.; Eight hundred and thirty-two Caster, Gold Inlaid, six four thousand seven hundred and thirty-two Bottles; One hundred and twenty Pickle; Two thousand one hundred nineteen and a half Chased Butter Dish; Two thousand eight hundred and six Chased Pudding Dish; One thousand two hundred and fifteen Fruit, Gold Inlaid and Colored Glass.

In ordering Flat Ware, each word indicates one dozen of the pattern it prefixes, in Extra Plate.

TEA SETS.
(ONE-THIRD SIZE.)

No. 1600.   TEA SET.   CHASED B.

Style, Chased,	Set of Six Pieces, $60.00. (ZONE)	Coffee, $12.50.	Tea, six half pints, $11.50.	Water, five half pints, $11.00.	Sugar, $8.00.	Cream, Gold Lined, $9.00.	Slop, Gold Lined, $8.00.

Without Gold Lining, $4.00 less.
No. 608.   Waiter, Chased B, 26 inch, $60.00.

No. 1600.   Urn.
Chased, $32.00.   (ZETA)

No. 1600.   Syrup.
Chased, with Plate, $7.50.   (ZAIN)

No. 1600.   Butter Dish.
Chased, $9.50.   (ZEAL)

No. 1600.   Spoon Holder.
Chased, Gold Lined, $7.50.   (ZANY)
Chased, not Gold Lined, 6.75.   (ZAX)

No. 1601. TEA SET. CHASED A.

Styles,	Set of Six Pieces,	Coffee,	Tea, six half pints,	Water, five half pints,	Sugar,	Cream, Gold Lined,	Slop, Gold Lined,
Plain,	$50.00. (ZERO)	$11.50.	$9.20.	$8.28.	$6.90.	$7.52.	$6.60.
Chased A,	60.00. (ZEST)	12.50.	11.50.	11.00.	8.00.	9.00.	8.00.

Without Gold Lining, $4.00 less.

No. 632. Waiter, Chased A, 26 inch, $60.00.

No. 1601. Butter Dish.

Plain, $8.00. (ZEND)
Chased A,   9.50. (ZEA)

No. 1601. Urn.

Plain, $29.00. (ZED)
Chased A,   32.00. (ZEBU)

No. 1601. Syrup Cup.

Plain, with Plate, $6.50. (ZINC)
Chased A, with Plate,   7.50. (ZOUNDS)

No. 1601. Spoon Holder.

Plain, Gold Lined, $6.50. (ZHO)
Chased A, Gold Lined,   7.50. (ZION)
Without Gold Lining, $0.75 less.

No. 1604. TEA SET.

Styles,	Set of Six Pieces,	Coffee,	Tea, six half pints,	Water, five half pints,	Sugar,	Cream, Gold Lined,	Slop, Gold Lined,
Plain,	$54.00. (YEA)	$11.50.	$10.50.	$9.25.	$6.75.	$8.25.	$7.75.
Chased,	60.00. (YEAN)	12.50.	11.50.	11.00.	8.00.	9.00.	8.00.

Without Gold Lining, $4.00 less.

No. 607. Waiter, Egyptian Chased, 26 inch, $60.00.

No. 1604. Butter Dish.

Plain, $8.00. (YELL)
Chased, 9.00. (YEAR)

No. 1604. Urn.

Plain, $29.00. (YEAST)
Chased, 32.00. (YEARN)

No. 1604. Syrup Cup.

Plain, with Plate, $7.00. (YEDE)
Chased, with Plate, 8.00. (YEEL)

No. 1604. Spoon Holder.

Plain, Gold Lined, $6.50. (YELK)
Chased, Gold Lined, 7.50. (YELLOW)
Without Gold Lining, $0.75 less.

WAITERS.

(ONE-THIRD SIZE.)

No. 619.   Waiter.

Chased, 20 inch, $28.00.   (WARBLE)

The above Waiter furnished with assorted styles of Chasing to match Tea Sets.

28 inch, $60.00.   (WARD)   26 inch, $53.00.   (WASHY)   24 inch, $42.00.   (WASP)   16 inch, $17.00.   (WASTE)

Gold Inlaid, $10.00 extra.

No. 621.   Waiter.

Chased, Niello Gold, 26 inch, $65.00.   (WARFARE)

The above Waiter furnished with assorted styles of Chasing to match Tea Sets.

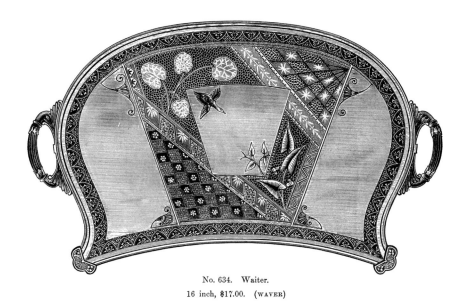

No. 634. Waiter.
16 inch, $17.00. (WAVER)

No. 607. Waiter.

Egyptian Chased, 28 inch, $65.00. (WEAL)　　26 inch, $60.00. (WEALTH)　　24 inch, $42.00. (WEAPON)　　20 inch, $28.00. (WEAR)　　16 inch, $17.00. (WEARY)
The above Waiter furnished with assorted styles of chasing to match Tea Sets.

No. 641. Waiter.

Chased, Niello Gold, 15 inch, $15.50. (WAR)

No. 615. Waiter.

Egyptian Chased, 15 inch, $13.50. (WEASEL)

No. 630.   Child's Tray.

Chased, 14 inches, $14.50.   (WAYLAY)

No. 1401.   Child's Plate.

Chased, $3.50.   (WEDGE)

No. 1402.   Child's Plate.

Chased, Niello Gold, $4.00.   (WEDDING)

No. 1400.   Child's Plate.

Chased, $3.50.   (WED)

No. 633.   Waiter.

Chased, 16 inch, $18.50.   (WAUL)

ICE PITCHER AND TILTING SETS.

(ONE-THIRD SIZE.)

No. 2005. Ice Pitcher Set.
Chased A, complete, $48.50. (WEFT)

No. 2005.	Pitcher,	$17.50.	(SALIENT)	No. 408.	Goblets, Gold Lined, each, $4.00. (SALLOW)
No. 608.	Waiter, 16 inch,	17.00.	(SALINE)	No. 4201.	Slop, Gold Lined, 6.00. (SALLY)

CHICAGO·ENG·CO

No. 02014. Tilting Pitcher Set, P. L.
Chased, Goblets and Slop Gold Lined, $58.00. (WEIGHT)

116

No. 02009½. Tilting Pitcher Set, P. L.
Goblets and Slop Gold Lined, $38.00. (WEIGH)

No. 2006. Ice Pitcher Set.

Chased A, complete, $51.50. (WELL)

No. 2006.	Pitcher, P. L., $18.50. (SAIL)	No. 409.	Goblets, Gold Lined, each, $4.50. (SAINT)
No. 608.	Waiter, 16 inch, 17.00. (SAILOR)	No. 4202.	Slop, Gold Lined, 7.00. (SAINTLY)

No. 02005½. Tilting Pitcher Set, P. L.

Chased, Goblets and Slop Gold Lined, $49.00. (WELLBRED)

No. 02018. Tilting Pitcher Set, P. L.

Chased, Goblets and Slop Gold Lined, $58.00. (WELSH)

No. 2022.   Ice Pitcher Set.

Chased, Niello Gold, complete, $48.25.   (WHERRY)

No. 2022.   Pitcher, P. L., $21.00.   (WHIFF)   No. 410.   Goblet, $4.75.   (WHEY)
No. 615.   Waiter, 15 inch, 15.50.   (WHIG)   No. 4204.   Slop,   7.00.   (WHICH)

No. 2018.   Ice Pitcher Set.

Chased, Gilt, complete, $50.75.   (SANK)

No. 2018.   P. L. Pitcher, $18.50.   (WHILE)   No. 422.   Goblets, Gold Lined, each, $4.00.   (WHINE)
No. 631.   Waiter, 16 inch, 18.50.   (WHIM)   No. 4208.   Slop, Gold Lined,   5.75.   (WHIP)

CASTERS.

(ONE-THIRD SIZE.)

No. 830. Caster.

Hammered, Silver, 6 No. 4097 Bottles, $17.50. (WHOEVER)
Hammered, Silver, 6 No. 3741 Bottles, 15.50. (WHOLE)

No. 829. Caster.

Hammered, Gilt Inlaid, 6 No. 4097 Bottles, $19.50. (WHOLESALE)
Hammered, Gilt Inlaid, 6 No. 3741 Bottles, 17.50. (WHOLLY)

No. 834. Caster.

Plain, Silver, 6 No. 4732 Bottles, $17.00. (WHITHER)

No. 832. Caster.

Silver,   6 No. 4732 Bottles, $15.50. (WHITTLE)
Gold Inlaid, 6 No. 4732 Bottles, 17.00. (WHIZ)

No. 912. Caster.

3 No. 3399 Bottles, $6.75. (WOLF)

No. 913. Caster.

2 No. 3399 Bottles, $4.50. (WITHER)

No. 828. Caster.

Plain, Silver, 6 No. 4097 Bottles, $9.50. (WIN)
Plain, Silver, 6 No. 3741 Bottles, 7.50. (WINCE)
Fancy Gilt, $1.00 extra.

No. 814. Caster.

Chased, 5 No. 3741 Bottles, $7.00. (WINTER)
Chased, 6 No. 3741 Bottles, 7.50. (WIPE)
Chased, 6 No. 4097 Bottles, 9.50. (WIRE)
Chased, 5 No. 4097 Bottles, 9.00. (WIRY)

No. 813. Caster.

Chased, 6 No. 4097 Bottles, $11.00. (WINDLASS)
Chased, 6 No. 3741 Bottles, 9.00. (WINE)
With Bell Handle, $1.50 extra.

No. 901. Caster.

Plain, 3 No. 3399 Bottles, $6.75. (WISEACRE)

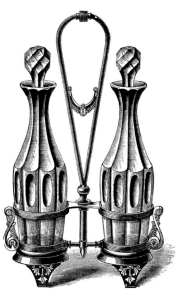

No. 2700. Salad Caster.

Oil and Vinegar, $13.50. (WISP)

No. 901. Caster.

3 No. 209 Bottles, $5.75. (WON)

No. 2702. Salad Caster.

Oil and Vinegar, $15.00. (WONDER.)

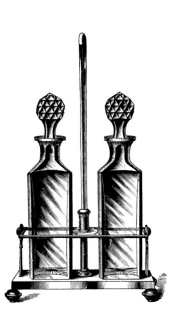

No. 2701. Salad Caster.

Oil and Vinegar, $15.00. (WIT)

CASTER BOTTLES AND HANDLES.

(ONE-THIRD SIZE.)

No. 4097. Bottle. (WONT)

No. 208. Bottle. (WOOL)

No. 208½. Bottle. (WOOD)

No. 3741. Bottle. (WOODLAND)

No. 628. Bottle.

(TWILL)

No. 3399. Bottle.

(WOOLLY)

No. 209. Bottle.

(WOOER)

Square Bottle.

(WOOF)

No. 1. Bell Handle.
$3.00. (WORD)
Extra List.

No. 2. Bell Handle.
$3.00. (WORLD)
Extra List.

No. 3. Bell Handle.
$3.00. (WOOLD)

No. 4. Vase Handle.
$2.50. (WORK)
Extra List.

No. 5. Vase Handle.
$2.50. (WORM)
Extra List.

Casters sold with these Handles charged extra as above.

PEPPERS, SALTS, VINEGARS, MUSTARDS, ETC.

(PEPPERS ONE-HALF SIZE. MUSTARDS AND VINEGARS ONE-THIRD SIZE.)

No. 710. Pepper.

Silver, $2.25. (TWIST)
Gilt,   2.50. (TWIT)

No. 710. Vinegar.

Silver, $2.00. (TWINKLE)
Gilt,   2.25. (TWIRL)

No. 710. Mustard.

Silver, $2.25. (SADDLE)
Gilt,   2.50. (SADLY)

No. 709. Pepper.

Silver, $3.75. (SAFE)
Gilt,   4.00. (SAG)

No. 709. Vinegar.

Silver, $3.50. (TYPE)
Gilt,   3.75. (TYRANT)

No. 709. Mustard.

Silver, $3.75. (TWINE)
Gilt,   4.00. (TWINGE)

No. 708. Pepper.

Silver, $2.50. (SACRED)
Gilt,   2.75. (SAD)

No. 708. Mustard.

Silver, $2.50. (TWITCH)
Gilt,   2.75. (TWITTER)

No. 708. Vinegar.

Silver, $2.25. (SABLE)
Gilt,   2.50. (SACK)

(ONE-THIRD SIZE.)

No. 705. Pepper.

Hammered, Silver, $1.75. (TORPOR)
Hammered, Gilt, 2.00. (TORRENT)

(FULL SIZE.)

(ONE-THIRD SIZE.)

No. 3435. Sugar Sifter.

Plain, $4.00. (TORRID)
Chased, 4.50. (SCALE)

No. 212. Salt.

Decorated Malachite Glass, $2.50. (TORTOISE)

(ONE-THIRD SIZE.)

No. 706. Muffineer.

Satin, Chased, $4.75. (TORT)

(ONE-HALF SIZE.)

No. 3425. Mustard.

Hammered, Silver, $5.00. (TORTURE)

(ONE-HALF SIZE.)

No. 3414. Mustard.

Satin, Chased, $5.50. (TORY)

(ONE-HALF SIZE.)

No. 3426. Mustard.

Embossed, Silver, $5.25. (TOSS)

PICKLE CASTERS.

(ONE-THIRD SIZE.)

No. 112.   Pickle Caster.
$4.50.   (WORSE)

No. 116.   Pickle Caster.
$6.50.   (WRATH)

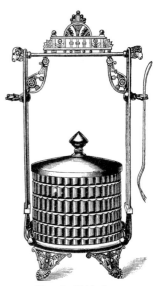

No. 132.   Pickle Caster.
Oval Glass, $8.50.   (WRAP)

No. 109.   Pickle Caster.
$9.50.   (WRECK)

No. 108.   Pickle Caster.
$4.50.   (WORST)

No. 130.   Pickle Caster.
$11.50.   (WRITHE)

No. 119.   Pickle Caster.
$4.75.   (WORTH)

No. 120.   Pickle Caster.
$6.75.   (WRINKLE)

No. 104.   Pickle Caster.
$3.50.   (WORTHY)

No. 126.   Pickle Caster.
$5.25.   (WRENCH)

No. 125.   Pickle Caster.
$6.50.   (WREST)

No. 118.   Pickle Caster.
$5.00.   (WORSHIP)

TOILET SETS.

(ONE-THIRD SIZE.)

No. 1933. Toilet Set.
Silver and Gold Inlaid, $26.00. (WROTE)

No. 1940. Toilet Set.
Silver and Gold Inlaid, $22.50. (VAGRANT)

No. 1914. Toilet Set.
Silver, $14.50. (VAGABOND)

No. 1917. Toilet Set.
Silver, $5.50. (VALE)

No. 1937. Scent Jar.
Silver and Gold Inlaid, $24.00. (VALET)

No. 1925. Toilet Set.
Silver, $9.50. (VALIANT)

No. 1934. Toilet Set.
Silver and Gold Inlaid, $24.00. (WRONG)

VASES.

(ONE-THIRD SIZE.)

No. 1332. Vase.
Silver and Gold Inlaid, $18.00. (VANISH)

No. 1331. Vase.
Silver and Gold, $13.50. (VANDYKE)

No. 4900. Jardinière.
Silver and Gold Inlaid, $28.00. (VANTAGE)

No. 1345. Vase.
Silver and Gold, $6.50. (VAN)

No. 1341. Vase.
Silver and Gold Inlaid, $16.50. (VANITY)

No. 1348. Vase.
Silver and Gold, $12.50. (VALID)

No. 1335. Vase.
Silver and Gold, $15.00. (VALISE)

No. 1342. Vase.
Silver and Gold, $25.00. (VALUE)

No. 1330. Vase.
Silver and Gold Inlaid, $16.50. (VALVE)

No. 1339. Vase.
Silver and Gold Inlaid, $20.00. (VALOR)

No. 1336. Vase.

Silver and Gold Inlaid, $8.00. (VARY)

No. 1352. Vase.

Silver and Gold, $10.50. (VAULT)

No. 1344. Vase.

Silver and Gold, $6.00. (VARNISH)

No. 1347. Vase.

Silver and Gold, $7.50. (VAMP)

No. 1343. Vase.

Silver and Gold, $9.00. (VALLEY)

No. 1337. Vase.

Silver and Gold, $8.50. (VAST)

No. 1333. Vase.

Silver and Gold, $10.00. (VATICAN)

No. 1349. Vase.

Silver and Gold Inlaid, $11.00. (VAT)

CAKE BASKETS.

(ONE-THIRD SIZE.)

No. 1025. Cake Basket.

Chased, Silver, $10.50.   (VENGEANCE)
Chased, Niello and Gold, 13.50.   (VENIAL)

No. 1012. Cake Basket.

Plain, Silver, $6.00.   (VESTAL)
Chased, Silver,   7.00.   (VESTIGE)
Chased, Niello and Gold, 10.00.   (VETERAN)

No. 1017. Cake Basket.
Plain, Silver, $6.50.   (VENT)

No. 1027. Cake Basket.

Chased, Niello and Gold, $15.50.   (VENTURE)

No. 1010. Cake Basket.

Plain, $7.00.   (VIGNETTE)
Chased,   8.00.   (VIGOR)

No. 1006. Cake Basket.

Plain, Silver,	$5.75.	(VICTOR)
Plain, Gold Lined,	7.75.	(VIE)
Chased, Silver,	6.25.	(VIEW)
Chased, Gold Lined,	8.25.	(VIGIL)

No. 1014. Cake Basket.

Plain, Silver,	$6.00.	(VEST)
Plain, Gold Lined,	8.00.	(VESPER)
Chased, Silver,	7.00.	(VERY)
Chased, Gold Lined,	9.00.	(VERSED)
Chased, Niello and Gold,	10.00.	(VERNAL)

No. 1019. Cake Basket.

Chased, Niello and Gold, $13.00. (VERANDA)

No. 1020. Cake Basket.

Chased, Silver,	$10.00.	(VERBAL)
Chased, Niello and Gold,	13.00.	(VERB)

BUTTER DISHES.

(ONE-THIRD SIZE.)

No. 2121. Butter Dish.
Plain, $9.75. (VITAL)
Chased, 10.50. (VIVID)

No. 2128. Butter Dish.
Plain, $8.25. (VILLAIN)
Chased, 9.00. (VILLAGE)

No. 2119½. Butter Dish.
Plain, $5.50. (VIOL)
Chased, 6.50. (VINE)

No. 2127. Butter Dish.
Plain, $7.75. (VIRGO)
Chased, 8.25. (VIRTUE)

No. 2124. Butter Dish.
Plain, $9.50. (VOCAL)
Chased, 10.50. (VOCATION)

No. 2134. Butter Dish.
Plain, $8.00. (VIOLIN)
Chased, 8.75. (VIPER)

No. 2112. Butter Dish.
Chased, $9.50. (VISOR)

No. 1606. Butter Dish.
Plain, $8.00. (WAIT)
Chased, 9.00. (WAG)

No. 2111. Butter Dish.
Chased, $8.75. (VIXEN)

No. 2118. Butter Dish.
Plain, $4.50. (VOLATILE)
Chased, 5.50. (VOID)

No. 2120. Butter Dish.
Plain, $6.50. (VOTE)

No. 2116. Butter Dish.
Plain, $4.50. (VULTURE)
Chased, 5.50. (VULCAN)

No. 1603. Butter.
Plain, $7.00. (YANK)
Chased, 7.75. (YAM)

No. 1607. Butter Dish.
Plain, $7.75. (VISIT)

SPOON HOLDERS.

(ONE-HALF SIZE.)

No. 3106.   Spoon Holder.

Chased, $5.00.   (UNCUT)
Chased, Gold Lined, 5.75.   (UNDER)

No. 3114.   Spoon Holder.

Chased, Gold Lined, $6.50.   (UNCTION)

No. 3106.   Spoon Holder.

Plain, $4.25.   (UNCLE)
Plain, Gold Lined, 5.00.   (UNCLOSE)

No. 3117.   Spoon Holder.

Chased, Gold Lined, with Bell, $8.00.   (UNCAGE)

No. 3118.   Spoon Holder.

Chased, Gold Lined, with Bell, $7.00.   (UNCHAIN)

No. 3105.   Spoon Holder.

Chased, $4.50.   (UNCOMMON)
Chased, Gold Lined, 5.25.   (UNCOUTH)

No. 3110.   Spoon Holder.

Chased, Gold Lined, $8.75.   (UNFADED)

No. 3105.   Spoon Holder.

Plain, $3.75.   (UNCOIL)
Plain, Gold Lined, 4.50.   (UNCOMELY)

(ONE-THIRD SIZE.)

No. 3121.   Spoon Holder.

Plain, $4.50.   (UNDERLAY)
Plain, Gold Lined,   5.25.   (UNDERRATE)
Chased,   5.25.   (UNDERSELL)
Chased, Gold Lined, 6.00.   (UNDERSHOT)

No. 3127.   Spoon Holder.

Chased, Gold Lined, $7.25.   (UNFURL)

No. 1603.   Spoon Holder.

Plain, Gold Lined, $5.50.   (YARN)
Plain, without Gold Lining,   4.50.   (YATE)
Chased, Gold Lined,   6.50.   (YARE)
Chased, without Gold Lining,   5.50.   (YARK)

No. 3128.   Spoon Holder.

Fancy, Gold and Gold Lined, $7.75.   (UNHAPPY)

No. 3126.   Spoon Holder.

Chased, Niello and Gold, $8.50.   (UNHAND)

No. 3120.   Spoon Holder.

Embossed, $4.25.   (UNDERSTAND)
Embossed, Gold Lined,   5.00.   (UNDERTAKE)

No. 1607.   Spoon Holder.

Plain, Silver Lined, $5.00.   (UNIVERSE)
Plain, Gold Lined,   6.00.   (UNIT)

No. 3122.   Spoon Holder.

Plain, $4.50.   (UNDO)
Plain, Gold Lined,   5.25.   (UNEASY)
Chased,   5.25.   (UNEQUAL)
Chased, Gold Lined, 6.00.   (UNEVEN)

No. 1601.   Spoon Holder.

Plain, Gold Lined, $6.50.   (ZHO)
Plain, without Gold Lining,   5.75.   (UNHEARD)
Chased A, Gold Lined,   7.50.   (ZION)
Chased, without Gold Lining,   6.75.   (UNHINGE)

No. 3123.   Spoon Holder.

Plain, $4.00.   (UNDERBID)
Plain, Gold Lined,   4.75.   (UNDERGO)

No. 3125.   Spoon Holder.

Embossed, $4.75.   (UNFIX)
Embossed, Gold Lined,   5.50.   (UNFOUNDED)

No. 3124.   Spoon Holder.

Embossed, $4.50.   (UNFAIR)
Embossed, Gold Lined,   5.25.   (UNFELT)

SOUP TUREENS.

(ONE-THIRD SIZE.)

No. 3705.   Soup Tureen.

Plain, 12 half pints, $15.00.   (UNPROP)

No. 3706.   Soup Tureen.

Plain, 8 half pints, $12.00.   (UNRIPE)

No. 3703.   Soup Tureen.   (Individual.)

Plain, $7.50.   (UNMADE)
Plain, with Plate, 9.00.   (UNMASK)

No. 3701.   Soup Tureen.

Chased B, $25.00.   (UNPACK)

No. 3704.   Soup Tureen.

Plain, $21.00.   (UNPEG)
Chased, 24.00.   (UNPIN)

PUDDING DISHES.

(ONE-THIRD SIZE.)

No. 2804. Pudding Dish.

Plain,   9½ inch, 8 half pints, $14.50. (UNJUST)
Chased, 9½ inch, 8 half pints, 16.50. (UNKIND)

No. 2806. Pudding Dish.

Plain,   9½ inch, 8 half pints, $13.50. (UNKNOT)
Chased, 9½ inch, 8 half pints, 15.50. (UNLACE)

No. 2805. Pudding Dish.

Plain,   9½ inch, 8 half pints, $15.50. (UNLEARN)
Chased, 9¼ inch, 8 half pints, 17.50. (UNLIKE)

No. 2803. Pudding Dish.

Plain,   9¼ inch, 8 half pints, $12.50. (UNLOAD)
Chased, 9¼ inch, 8 half pints, 14.00. (UNLUCKY)

NAPKIN RINGS.

(FULL SIZE.)

No. 349. Napkin Ring.

Chased, Silver, per doz., $12.00. (TAUGHT)
Chased, Gold Inlaid, per doz.,   15.00. (TAURUS)
Chased, Gold Inlaid and Gold Lined, per doz., 18.00. (TAVERN)

No. 328. Napkin Ring.

Chased, Silver, each, $2.00. (TEPID)

No. 326. Napkin Ring.

Chased, Silver, each, $1.50. (TAN)
Chased, Gold, each,   2.00. (TANGLE)

No. 314. Napkin Ring.

Plain, per doz., $6.00. (TASTE)
Chased, per doz., 7.00. (TATTLE)

No. 355. Napkin Ring.

Chased, Silver, per doz., $7.50. (TEACH)
Chased, Gold, per doz.,   10.50. (TEAM)
Chased, Niello Gold, Gold Lined, per doz., 13.50. (TEASE)

No. 337. Napkin Ring.

Chased, per doz., $9.00. (TALLY)

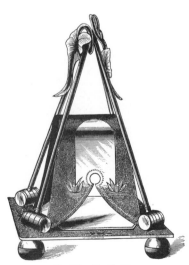

No. 302. Napkin Ring.

Chased, Silver, each, $1.20. (TEMPEST)

No. 303. Napkin Ring.

Chased, each, $1.20. (TABBY)

No. 304. Napkin Ring.

Chased, Silver, each, $1.20. (TENDON)

No. 344. Napkin Ring.

Chased, Silver, each, $1.50. (TALL)
Chased, Gold, each,   2.00. (TALLOW)

No. 352. Napkin Ring.

Chased, per doz., $8.00. (TARDY)
Chased, Gold, per doz.,   11.00. (TARIFF)
Chased, Gold and Gold Lined, per doz., 14.00. (TARNISH)

No. 343. Napkin Ring.

Chased, Silver, each, $1.50. (TACK)
Chased, Gold, each,   2.00. (TACT)

No. 339. Napkin Ring.

Chased, each, $7.50. (TALON)

No. 324. Napkin Ring.

Chased, Silver, per doz., $9.50. (TENNIS)
Chased, Niello Gold, per doz.,   12.50. (TENSE)
Chased, Niello Gold and Gold Lined, per doz., 15.50. (TENT)

No. 313. Napkin Ring.

Plain, per doz., $5.00. (TABLE)

No. 347. Napkin Ring.

Chased, Silver, each, $1.50. (TAME)
Chased, Gold, each,   2.00. (TAMPER)

No. 308. Napkin Ring.

Chased, Silver, per doz., $15.00. (TAX)
Chased, Niello and Gold, per doz.,   18.00. (TEA)
Chased, Niello Gold and Gold Lined, per doz., 21.00. (TEAPOT)

No. 340. Napkin Ring.

Chased, Silver, each, $1.50. (TAKE)
Chased, Gold, each,   2.00. (TALK)

No. 335.   Napkin Ring.

Chased, each, $1.25.   (TEMPLAR)
Chased, Niello Gold, each,   1.50.   (TEMPT)
Chased, Niello Gold and Gold Lined, each, 1.75.   (TENANT)

No. 342.   Napkin Ring.

Chased, Silver, Vase, Gold Lined, each, $2.75.   (TAG)

No. 334.   Napkin Ring.

Chased, Silver, each, $2.00.   (TEND)

No. 345.   Napkin Ring.

Chased, Silver, each, $1.50.   (TENDRIL)
Chased, Gold, each,   2.00.   (TENET)

No. 329.   Napkin Ring.

Chased, each, $1.25.   (TANK)
Chased, Niello and Gold, each, 1.50.   (TANNER)

No. 346.   Napkin Ring.

Chased, each, $1.50.   (TELL)
Chased, Gold, each, 2.00.   (TEMPER)

INDIVIDUAL CASTERS.

(ONE-HALF SIZE.)

No. 509. Individual Caster.

Chased, Gold, $5.50. (THINK)

No. 507. Individual Caster.

Chased, Gold, $5.50. (THAW)

No. 505½. Individual Caster.

Chased, Gold, $5.25. (THATCH)

No. 506. Individual Caster.

Chased, Gold, $5.75. (THEFT)

No. 512. Individual Caster.

Chased, $6.00. (TEXTILE)
Chased, with Ring, 6.75. (THAN)

No. 508. Individual Caster.

Chased, Gold, $6.00. (THAT)

No. 510. Individual Caster.

Chased, Gold, $6.00. (THANK)

CARD RECEIVERS.

(ONE-THIRD SIZE.)

No. 3519.   Card Receiver.

Chased, Niello and Gold, $8.00.   (THEREIN)

No. 3520.   Card Receiver.

Chased, Niello and Gold, $8.50.   (THERE)

No. 3513.   Card Receiver.

Chased, Silver, $7.00.   (THEIR)
Chased, Niello and Gold, 8.00.   (THEIST)

No. 3516.   Card Receiver.

Chased, Gold, $7.50.   (THEM)

No. 3521.   Card Receiver.

Chased, Niello and Gold, $10.00.   (THEORY)

No. 3522.   Card Receiver.

Chased, Niello and Gold, $7.50.   (THEREBY)

No. 3518.   Card Receiver.

Chased, Niello Gold, $5.50.   (THIEF)

No. 3515.   Card Receiver.

Chased, Niello and Gold, $7.25.   (THEY)

No. 3511.   Card Receiver.

Chased, Gold, $6.00.   (THICK)

No. 3526.   Card Receiver.

Chased, Niello and Gold, $12.00.   (THILL)
Decorated Porcelain.

No. 3524.   Card Receiver.

Chased, Gold, $9.00.   (THESE)

No. 3523.   Card Receiver.

Chased, Niello and Gold, $10.50.   (THENCE)

No. 3527.   Card Receiver.

Chased, Silver, $5.50.   (THIMBLE)

FRUIT STANDS.

(ONE-THIRD SIZE.)

No. 1210.   Fruit Stand.
Chased, Gold Inlaid, $19.50.   (THORN)

No. 1216.   Fruit Stand.
Gold Inlaid, Colored Glass, $18.00.   (THRASH)

No. 1208.   Fruit Stand.
Chased, Gold, $40.00.   (THIN)

No. 1209.   Fruit Stand.
Chased, Gold Inlaid, Decorated Glass, $38.00.   (THONG)

No. 1204.   Fruit Stand.

Chased, Gold Lined, $25.00.   (THIRD)

No. 1206.   Fruit Stand.

Chased, Gold Lined, $25.00.   (THIRST)

No. 1214.   Fruit Stand.

Chased, Silver Lined, $16.50.   (THIS)
Chased, Gold Lined and Inlaid, 19.50.   (THISTLE)

No. 1211.   Fruit Stand.

Chased, Silver Lined, $18.00.   (THOSE)
Chased, Gold Lined,   20.00.   (THOU)

BERRY DISHES.

(ONE-THIRD SIZE.)

No. 3216. Berry Dish.
Chased, Silver and Gold, Decorated Glass, $28.00. (THRONG)

No. 3215. Berry Dish.
Gold Inlaid, Decorated Glass, $16.50. (THRONE)

No. 3204. Berry Dish.
Chased, Silver, $24.50. (THRICE)

CUPS.

(ONE-HALF SIZE.)

No. 45. Cup.

Plain, Gold Lined, $2.50. (THWART)
Chased, Gold Lined, 3.00. (SCOUR)

No. 55. Cup.

Hammered, Silver, Gold Lined, $3.50. (TICK)
Hammered, Gold Inlaid, Gold Lined, 4.00. (TICKET)
Hammered, Oxidized, Gold Lined,   3.75. (TICKLE)

No. 48. Cup.

Chased, Silver Lined, $2.50. (TIARA)

No. 58. Cup.

Chased, Gold Lined, $3.75. (TIERCE)

No. 56. Cup.

Hammered, Silver, Gold Lined, $3.50. (TIDBIT)
Hammered, Gold Inlaid, Gold Lined, 4.00. (TIDE)
Hammered, Oxidized, Gold Lined,   3.75. (TIDY)

No. 50. Cup.

Chased, Gold Lined, $3.25. (TIFF)

No. 59. Cup.

Plain, Silver Lined, $2.75. (TIGER)
Chased, Silver Lined, 3.25. (SCOURGE)

No. 61. Cup.

Plain, Silver Lined, $2.00. (TIGHT)
Chased, Silver Lined, 2.50. (SCOUT)

No. 62. Cup.

Chased, Niello, Gold Lined, $4.00. (TIKE)

GOBLETS.

(ONE-HALF SIZE.)

No. 406. Goblet.

Chased, Gold Lined, $4.00. (TOLL)

No. 425. Goblet.

Hammered, Chased, Gold Lined, $4.50. (TOKEN)

No. 421. Goblet.

Chased, Gold Lined, $3.25. (TOD)

No. 411. Prize Goblet.

Chased, Niello Gold, $35.00. (TOLD)

No. 412. Goblet.

Chased, Gold Lined, $3.50. (TINKER)

No. 414. Goblet.

Chased, Gold Lined, $4.00. (TIRADE)

No. 410. Goblet.

Chased, Niello, Gold Lined, $4.00. (TOMB)

SYRUPS.

(ONE-THIRD SIZE.)

No. 3006. Syrup.

Embossed, with Plate, $7.25. (TOP)

No. 1605. Syrup.

Plain, with Plate, $6.50. (WIZEN)
Chased, with Plate, 7.50. (WITTOL)

No. 3008. Syrup.

Plain, with Plate, $7.00. (TOPPLE)
Chased, with Plate, 7.75. (TOPIC)

No. 3005. Syrup.

Hammered, Silver, with Plate, $6.75. (TOPER)

No. 3004. Syrup.

Hammered, Silver, with Plate, $7.00. (TORCH)

No. 1600. Syrup.

Chased, with Plate, $7.50. (ZAIN)

No. 1604. Syrup.

Plain, with Plate, $7.00. (YEDE)
Chased, with Plate, 8.00. (YEEL)

No. 1601. Syrup.

Plain, with Plate, $6.50. (ZINC)
Chased A, with Plate, 7.50. (ZOUNDS)

SUGARS AND CREAMS.

(ONE-THIRD SIZE.)

No. 1123. Cream.
Hammered, Chased, Gold Lined, $7.75. (TOWAGE)

No. 1106. Sugar.
Ruby Glass, Silver, with Spoons, $12.75. (TRANSACT)
Ruby Glass, Silver, without Spoons, 8.00. (TRANSFER)

No. 1120. Cream.
Embossed, Gold Lined, $6.00. (TOWN)

No. 1123. Sugar.
Hammered, Chased, Gold Lined, $7.50. (TOWARD)

No. 1120. Sugar.
Embossed, Gold Lined, $6.25. (TOWER)

No. 1118. Cream.
Silver, Gold, Decorated Ruby Glass, $8.50. (TOW)

No. 1121. Cream.
Chased, Gold Lined, $6.50. (TRAGEDY)

No. 1117. Cream.
Chased, Gold Lined, $5.75. (TRAFFIC)

No. 1118. Sugar.
Silver, Fancy Gold, Decorated Ruby Glass, $9.50. (TOUR)

No. 1121. Sugar.
Chased, Gold Lined, $6.75. (TOUSE)

No. 1117. Sugar.
Chased, Gold Lined, $5.50. (TOURIST)

NUT BOWLS.

(ONE-THIRD SIZE.)

No. 4800.   Nut Bowl.
Chased, Silver, Gold Lined, $26.00.   (TREAD)

No. 4000.   Epergne.
Silver, Gold Lined, Decorated Coral Glass, $48.00.   (TREASURE)

No. 4801.   Nut Bowl.
Chased, Gold Lined, $21.50.   (TREASON)

153

EPERGNES.

(ONE-THIRD SIZE.)

No. 4004. Epergne.

Gold Inlaid, Niello Gold Lined, Decorated Coral Glass, $58.00. (TREAT)

ASH RECEIVERS, PUFF AND SARDINE BOXES, ETC.

(ONE-THIRD SIZE.)

No. 1508.   Ash Receiver.
Silver, Gold Lined, $5.50.   (TRELLIS)

No. 4501.   Puff Box.
Gold Lined, $5.00.   (TRENCH)

No. 2301.   Toothpick Holder.
Chased, Gold Lined, $2.50.   (ORATOR)

No. 1507.   Ash Receiver.
Gold Lined, $5.50.   (TRESTLE)

No. 2300.   Toothpick Holder.
Chased, Gold Lined, $3.50.   (TRESS)

No. 4500.   Puff Box.
Chased, Gold Lined, $3.50.   (TRET)

No. 1505.   Ash Receiver.
Chased, Gold Lined, $6.50.   (TREND)

No. 3410.   Shaving Mug.
Plain, Silver Lined, $4.00.   (TRIAL)
Chased, Silver Lined,   4.75.   (TRIBE)
Plain, Gold Lined,   4.75.   (TRICK)
Chased, Gold Lined,   5.50.   (TRICE)

No. 4100.   Sardine Box.
Chased, Silver, $10.50.   (TRIAD)

KNIFE RESTS.

(FULL SIZE.)

No. 3300. Knife Rest.

Silver, per dozen, $7.50. (TRICKLE)

No. 3301. Knife Rest.

Per dozen, $9.00. (TRIDENT)

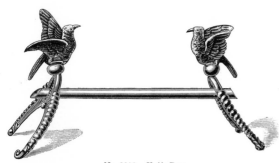

No. 3303. Knife Rest.

Silver, per dozen, $12.50. (TRIFLE)

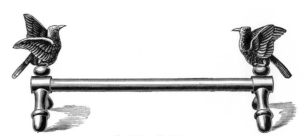

No. 3302. Knife Rest.

Per dozen, $10.50. (TRIER)

No. 3304. Knife Rest.

Silver, per dozen, $14.00. (TRIG)